A Memoir

ELEMENTARY, MY DEAR

)

K. BETHANY

K.BETHANY & KBW HOLDING LLC.

K. Bethany
Kbethany2018@gmail.com
Detroit, MI 48235

"Knowledge is infinite, my words are my Melody and Wisdom is the lyrics to the keys of my soul!"-K. Bethany

For my mother, Annie Ruth Wade. You were one of the greatest representations of God that blessed this realm with a magnificent zeal of light, I'm forever grateful for you.

PROLOGUE

I ran down the street soaking wet from the sweat of nervousness that I felt. My heart was beating uncontrollably, I was so afraid. I felt as if I was going into cardiac arrest, all of this factored in with the elements. I looked over my shoulder as the sleet struck my face like shards of wet glass. I could hear the sound of my sister's voice getting louder and louder as she gained momentum *"YOU GOT ON MY JACKET? I'M GOING TO KILL YOU WHEN I CATCH YOU! YOU'RE DEAD KIM! DO YOU HEAR ME? YOUR ASS IS DEAD!"* shouted Shay. Yes, I could hear her loud and clear, maybe I shouldn't have done it but I did. There was no turning back now. My sister Shay was closer now, a lot closer than she had been moments ago. I continued to run with great speed, trying my damnedest to get away… *NO!!!* Stay away from her and the pain that she would inflict upon my body. This was just another day in my life of… *Elementary, My Dear*!

Before I get into why I was being chased by my sister or running for my life, I have to take you back to how this all began. As far back as I can remember, I have always hated things that didn't have anything to do with me having fun. I loved playing games, watching cartoons, eating *Froot Loops*, ice cream, candy and cake. I enjoyed anything that would and could make a child feel happy, euphoric even. *FUN!!!* Fun, more fun and good times was what I was all about. However, there was something that I never wanted to experience, that was the big *"S"* word... *SCHOOL.* I hated school so much. I also hated the fact that summer had come to a close and it was now time for me to go back to this place that I dreaded so much. Now don't get me wrong, I would play pretend school with my friends and cousins but that was then and this is now. The tables have turned and I have decided that, *I AM NEVER GOING BACK THERE, THAT'S ALL TO IT!* It's just that, all everyone keeps talking about is school this and school that. No *ifs, ands* or *buts* about it. We all had to go and to me, this summer vacation shit didn't last long enough.

As I take a look back at my life, I can honestly convey to you that I hated school with a passion. From elementary school to middle school, high school and even college. I loathed any and everything that had to do with it. For me, school was nothing more than a prison sentence. It was just something about being in a classroom where someone could ask you to answer a question that you may not have the answer for, that always seemed to bother me. *Why put someone on the spot?* When you knew deep down inside, they didn't have the answer. *Hell*, they didn't even raise their hand nor did they make a gesture for you to call on them, *so why pick on them?* You really don't know if they were just shy, afraid or if they had even grasped the concept of what was being taught. My theory is that there is never a right or wrong answer, every answer is potentially correct and it just depends on who you're talking too. I have always been a firm believer that everyone does not learn on the same level. So, my question is, *How can a teacher who has been taught to teach in a particular style, using the 5 basic methods of teaching, continue to teach thirty plus students the same exact thing?* This seems rather impossible to me.

Wouldn't it be sort of mundane to teach them all on the same

accord? What the hell is a grade anyway? Just my thoughts.

When I think about the time that I was growing up, I can

honestly say that I was a very inquisitive child and was so full

of life. Although I was very shy when it came to strangers and

people I didn't know, when it came down to my family and

friends I could never shut up. I had many questions and I was

very eager for knowledge. You couldn't tell me nothing and I

thought I knew everything but I didn't. Whatever it was, I had

to know about it… *I needed to know about it!* I was never one

to pry *(so I thought)* but never was I ever inappropriate.

Although, I would always get caught trying to listen in on

conversations that did not concern me, so I guess you could say

I pried a bit. I wasn't old enough to have knowledge or wisdom

to understand the meaning of what they were always *gossiping*

about. My grandmother, who we called *MA'MA* would often

times say, *"MAKE HASTE AND GET OUT OF HERE! This*

conversation doesn't concern you." While taking a long drag from the cigarette that parted her full lips. *"You are not grown and if I see your little narrow behind in here again trying to listen to grown up conversation, you're not going to like the outcome. Now get on outta here! Cause' if you don't, I'm going to get a switch off of that bush out there and beat your little black ass!"*

CHAPTER 1

LIFE AS I KNEW IT

"Smell and sense everything that is around you, it's true soul love!"

As I close my eyes, I reminisce back on those beautiful hot summer days. I can still smell the lighter fluid being pored over the fire blazed charcoal on the grill. Everyone dancing to *Song's in the Key of Soul* being played by the local neighborhood band *The Montego's*, with their *Afro-Latin Funk* with a hint of *Jazz* persuasion, all being done in our community backyard. Everyone would gather around talking, laughing, while the children would be playing, these were all good times.

My early childhood life began on the North End of Detroit, Michigan. An area that used to be apart of a prominent dueling black community located in the center of the city called, *Paradise Valley* and *Black Bottom*. By the twentieth century, this area was a vibrant business and entertainment district that established a solid foundation of black culture. With its many doctor's offices, hospitals, grocery stores and other prominent businesses, success wasn't to far from reach. Not only were there prominent black businesses and owners, there were very successful black nightclubs that frequently supported the rising careers of great *Jazz* and *Blues* musicians from all over such as, *Billie Holiday*, *Ella Fitzgerald*, *Duke Ellington*, *Donald Byrd*, *Pearl Bailey*, *Count Basie* and the list goes on and on. As quickly as this prominent black area experienced an economic boom, it felt the sabotaging blows of forced segregation by ways of redlining, housing and urban development projects, poverty and *white flight*. The 1950's green lighted interstate freeways to be ran through prominent black areas and the North End felt the brunt of the storm. By the mid-1960's the

14

prominence that once was *Paradise Valley* and *Black Bottom* were mere moments lost within a mirage that seemed to fade along interstate 375.

Around the time that I came of age to attend school, the North End was quite different from its zenith of the past. Disconnected from center city and considered the northeast side of Detroit, The North End was just another ghetto and drug infested neighborhood along the Woodward corridor to some, *yet* you still had successful people who came from this area. Especially those who aspired to be singers or entertainers, like the artists who were with *Motown*. We had *Smokey Robinson, Diana Ross*, the *Four Tops* and even the great *Queen of Soul* herself, *Ms. Aretha Franklin* who also grew up on the North End of Detroit in our midst. You could always spot someone or some group singing on the corner, awaiting their big break. There was never a dull moment, especially in the household that I grew up in. Everybody wanted to be a star, including me and not to work in a factory or as someone's maid. So, my mother explained to me that in order for me to

achieve those dreams, I'd have to attend school (*even though I*

didn't want to).

The first school that I ever attended was Palmer Elementary

that was located not to far from where some of these

individuals lived or grew up. This gave hope to many families

in the community that one day, they too could make it. Though

this area wasn't the former glory that it once was, it was home

and the people that lived there were family. When I first started

school, I went straight to the kindergarten. There was no pre-

school or anything like that, you were just thrown in. This to

me, meant the end of my childhood as I knew it. There would

be no more staying up late at night, no more watching cartoons

all day, all of that would definitely have to come to an end. Just

as fast as I could blink an eye, those things did just that… they

ended. Reminiscing back when the first day of school was (*as

the adults would say*), *"Just around the corner"* there seemed

to be an unrest, something about the schools going on strike. I (*not really knowing what this all meant*) stood there and

listened to my grandmother *fuss* about it and from what I could

make out of this thing, it meant that there was a good chance

that none of us would be going to school. That was fine with

me, this meant more playtime and sleep.

It was a hot August day, almost time for my birthday and the

schools had been talking about striking all summer long. I

remember my grandmother calling her daughters in the room,

some still school age and some who were grown that were also

living with us with their entire families, all huddled up around

the black and white television with the bunny ears that you had

to turn with pliers, paying close attention to the afternoon

news. *"Annie Ruth, hurry up and get in here so you can see if*

the school is gone' be on strike!" My grandmother yelled to my

mother who was in the kitchen preparing lunch for the entire

family. My mom rushed out of the kitchen with an apron on

drying her hands with a kitchen towel. *"Hurry up and fix the*

damn picture!" MA'MA yelled as she sat in the *easy chair* in front of the television with her feet up, lighting and taking another long drag from a cigarette. While her lips formed into a circle so that she could blow rings of smoke through her mouth, I jumped in front of her to try catching the circles before they disappeared into the atmosphere. The television was messing up as usual, so my mom threw the kitchen towel on the table and ran over to the television, hitting it a couple of times on the top, the sides and adjusting the antenna to keep it from messing up. *"Please don't strike, get this girl out of my face! What's wrong with her?"* MA'MA exclaimed, pausing to take another drag from her cigarette. In the middle of blowing smoke from the corner of her mouth she hollered, *"Where is Debra? Tell her I said come and get these kids, so I can hear the television! These damn kids have got to go somewhere, they need to be in school. SHUT UP ALL THAT RACKET AND MAKE HASTE AND FIX THAT DAMN TV!"* I stood there continuing to look at my grandmother, while she tried to gain control of her house. I was in awe of how blue her eyes were, I couldn't help but stare at her. *"What are you looking at?"* MA'MA asked *"Annie Ruth come and get this girl! Get this*

18

child out of the way! Annie Ruth, did you hear me? This is your child, now get her and send her in there with Debra Ann and the rest of the kids. I'm tired of her staring at me. What's wrong with this child?" I saw the look in my grandmother's eyes. A look that I had become very accustomed to and I knew that she was not playing. *MA'MA* was *dead serious*, so I ran into the other room where my aunt Debra and the other children were and began listening to music.

MATTIE LEE

As far back as I can remember, I've always listened to my grandmother *cause'* she didn't play around. I know many of you could probably relate. If you ask me, she was the backbone of our entire family, *hell,* she was the glue that held the neighborhood together. Sitting there with her peach house dress on with the flowers on the bottom, her hair parted down the middle with a braid on each side, continued to demand and take control of all situations. My grandmother was the epitome of a strong black and beautiful woman. Even if she was taught not to believe that herself, in my eyes she was. Mattie Lee Wade (*MA'MA*), with her beautiful dark brown skin and her piercing bluish grey eyes was the tie that held it all together, no matter how dysfunctional things may have seemed. My grandmother didn't have a care for drama. To her, it *didn't matter who was arguing with who, who wasn't talking to who, who was the prostitutes, who went to jail, who just got out of jail, who was the drunk or who was the drug addict, who was pregnant, who had dreamt of fish and was going to be pregnant, who had a million kids and kept having them without being able to feed them, who's left ear was burning cause somebody was talking about them, who's right eye was jumping cause they were about to have good luck or who's hand was itching cause they were about to come into some money or who was going to sweep somebody out cause' they didn't want them in their home anymore.* None of those things mattered to her and because of that, she was the epitome of perfection in my eyes. Even though I'd never seen her crack a smile or even laugh for that matter, she was still perfection. *MA'MA* never passed judgement of anyone who had those issues or situations. She was always there to lend a helping hand. My grandmother always had a way of bringing people together. No matter how mean I thought she was at times, everyone always wanted to be around her. As a matter of fact, all it took was one phone call from her and just like that, everyone came together.

Although I could say a lot of great things about the way my grandmother was towards other people, there was another side of her that I couldn't quite come to grips with... and that was her perspective on dark complexion. Even though *MA'MA* was very dark skinned herself, she was a very color struck woman. For some, that could be a hard pill to swallow but growing up in the era of time that she did, made it very hard for her to be accepting of children who were born darker *than*. This way of thinking was the brutal result of abuse she'd suffered and the racial climate of the *Deep South* still being very thick and flagrant. If you had any hint of brownness or dark hue to your skin, she didn't think that you were beautiful, *hell* she didn't think that she was beautiful. This led me to believe that this was the very reason why she was accepting of such harsh treatment by many men.

That type of self inflicted hate was the very thing that made it hard for me to accept myself, as her judgment was felt by all of her *darker skinned* grandchildren. For *MA'MA* to be accepting of you, your complexion had to be very light and or (*as they would say back in the day*) high yellow. *How did this treatment make me feel, you might ask?* This treatment made me grow up believing that because my skin was a brown caramel color, I was lesser than some of my family members. Many of which, I felt were treated better than me because of how light *their* skin was. I not only believed they were treated better, I also believed they were given far more opportunities than me. In my mind, I knew that I needed to do something about that situation. My thoughts are simple yet massive, positive representation of who and what you look like matters and is very important. Especially for the young girls that look like me, who were blessed with melanin that showcases their brown or darker skin. Our self esteem depends heavily on this! *Did you know, I would walk around with a white sheet or towel on my head, pretending it was my hair? (which was a really sad situation)* I'd felt that if only I would have been born with long flowing blonde hair, blue eyes or even lighter skin she would love me; maybe then, just then I could also learn to love myself... too.

My Grandmother, with skin as dark as the night time sky and captivating eyes that were as blue as the deepest ocean, was of African and Seminole Indian descent. An indigenous heritage of *Maroons* compiled of *Tonkawa, Creek, Muskogee, Choctaw* and *Freedmen* wrapped into one. This distinctive group of

Native Americans were the product of enslaved Africans and the Indigenous Black Natives from several regions of the Carolinas and Georgia, who'd escaped slavery and ventured deeper south into northern Florida during *The Trail of Tears* also known as the *Seminole Wars*. They would go on to establish *maroon* colonies or safe sanctuaries for runaways who were fighting to be free from the hands of chattel slavery throughout the bordering states of the deepest points of the south and even the Bahamas. *MA'MA* was apart of that heritage as well as lineage and oftentimes showcased this sparingly throughout her life but with a heritage as foundational as that, *where could she have learned to feel this deep discontent from who she was and what she looked like?*

A DEEPER LOOK INTO THOSE BLUE EYES

My grandmother was born in the earlier part of the 1900's in the month of September, though based on several accounts no one truly knew when. I guess that old adage holds true, *a woman never reveals her true age.* The area that *MA'MA* grew up in was considered the *Deep South*, on a small farm that used to be apart of one of the largest cotton plantations in Antebellum Georgia, called Pavo. Ever since my grandmother was a young girl, she was forced to become a hardworking woman. *MA'MA* not only took good care of her many children, she also took care of other people's children as well. My grandmother had no other choice but to learn early on how to take care of others. This was partly due to her having her first child and becoming a mother just at the very tender age of 12, this was the harsh reality that many young black girls faced back in those days. One could only assume that she was very tired, tired of the pain she had

endured and tired of the life she had come to live.

In my eyes, my grandmother was very strong but if you were to

take a deeper look into her heavy blue eyes, you'd know that

this wasn't always the case. *MA'MA* had it harder than most

and this added scars and blemishes to her self worth. By the

time she was grown, she'd already endured the hardships of a

person twice her age or who had lived three lifetimes already.

From her suffering through the damaging psychological affects

of racism during the *Jim Crow Era*, to catching the same hell

within her own marriage. These factors would lead my

grandmother to a breaking point, a place that probably left her

feeling *numb* to the possibility of change or even something

better. To stay in that environment meant she was giving up or

even worse, preparing to die.

My grandmother had no other choice and like the ancestors

before her, fled the south. *MA'MA*, with some of her children in

tow and only the clothes on their backs, fled the segregated city of Moultrie Georgia. This was a daring *yet* risky attempt to escape an abusive husband that made her life as well as her children's life, a living hell. Even though my grandmother finally got up enough nerve to head north, it wouldn't be easy. Her roots were stretched beneath the soil of the deepest parts of Georgia. The small towns of Pavo, Moultrie and even Milledgeville Georgia, ran through her veins. To migrate and adjust to a city like Detroit, Michigan would serve its share of challenges.

I've heard stories of how my grandfather also known as Wade, hatred of *MA'MA* grew more intense once he'd found out that she had left him. I suspect that the feelings he had toward my grandmother could have stemmed from the deep racism that he also encountered, from the vantage point of being a black man of *mixed* race. Wade suffered from the symptoms of a *tragic mullato*, by having to endure stigmatic prejudices from both ends of the racial spectrum. This resulted in him becoming a very mean and surly man, as he didn't know where he stood in life.

Living in the southern most part of the country in those times, was a very hard and dangerous thing to do for black people and people who were of *mixed* race or *mullato*. The white men didn't accept my grandfather for being black *nor* did the black community accept him for having a white lineage either. Wade went through this pain of not knowing where to rightfully stand on a daily basis and for every ounce of turmoil he suffered through, he took and released that same amount of, *(if not more)* hatred onto my grandmother and their many children. There was no peace in their household... as there was no peace in my grandfather's heart.

Some of the stories that I was told by my aunt Grace, one of *MA'MA's* eldest children, about my grandfather's treatment of them was unbelievable. She said that even though my grandfather, *(who was her stepfather by the way)* owned land, a diner and was considered a *backwoods Doctor* by trade, they were treated very poorly. There was a time when they didn't even have shoes or a bed to sleep on and if it wasn't for my great grandmother Mary, who was an indigenous Seminole Indian, they would've never had any of those things. She told me that great grandma Mary made her and her siblings beds and shoes with her bare hands. Aunt Grace, who was about 80 years old at the time, stated that those beds that great grandma Mary made for them was the softest and most comfortable of any bed, that she had ever slept on in her entire life. I was also told by my Aunt Grace that if it were not for *MA'MA's* eldest sister Bertha, she would have stayed in Georgia with that man. One day, Aunt Bertha had enough of the abuse that my grandmother was enduring, so she took it upon herself that she was going to take *MA'MA* to the local train station when my grandfather was at work. I was told that Aunt Bertha had to do it this way because if it were up to my grandmother, she would have stayed with Wade and would have continued to endure all of that abuse and for what? *Tell me, where was the love? Where was the joy or the happiness of that relationship?* There was no love, joy or peace, only chaos in that situation. My grandmother couldn't recognize the reality of what was going

29

on because she was blinded by her own love for him. She'd grown numb and was in denial of the level of heartache my grandfather had put her through. *How could she have fully healed, if she didn't get away from him?* She loved him, despite the beatings, the cheating and the many outside children that she accepted and raised as her own, she still loved this man. I've heard stories of my aunt Bertha and great grandma Mary coming to *MA'MA's* rescue on several occasions brandishing guns and all, telling my grandfather *they would kill him dead* if he ever put his hands on my grandmother again; and yet... she stayed. The beatings continued up until the day Aunt Bertha had just about enough of my grandfather's abuse to her sister and her children. Aunt Bertha didn't mind helping my grandmother at all but she was growing tired of *MA'MA* running to her home with the children in hand, trying to escape my grandfather's abuse. This had become too much to bare, she knew my grandmother would go back to him without hesitation if she didn't do something to get her far away from him.

After many sleepless nights and falling to the lowest point in her life, her whole entire body aching from all of the abuse that she felt mentally and physically, deep down in her heart and soul she had no other choice but to make a change for herself as well as for her children. My grandmother had to change the way she looked at the big picture, so she became tired of being tired and ending up in the same situations. It took a lot of convincing from Aunt Bertha but she was able to convince *MA'MA* to finally leave the only home that she ever knew, with her two youngest children. Aunt Bertha felt that once enough money was raised, she would send the remaining children up north with my grandmother. Aunt Bertha purchased the train tickets for *MA'MA* and her younger children to go to Detroit. My grandmother learned that walking away from my grandfather for the last time was the best thing that she could have ever done. She learned that those who walked into her life to treat her mean were never meant to be there or stay. *MA'MA* knew that everyone who came into her life had a purpose and that lesson was to love her, not to break her. My grandfather may have thought that he was teaching her a lesson but in fact, her lesson had been learned and the most important gift that came from the chaos of there union, was the fruit that was bore between them, their children and the creation of my beautiful mother. Without that, there would be no me.

REFUGE UNDER A PEACH TREE

My grandmother successfully left the state of Georgia, it was a bittersweet feeling because the majority of her children still remained there. *MA'MA* never returned to Georgia to get them or for the remainder of her life. She wouldn't go to the many family reunions that we had to attend and if any of her family or friends wanted to see her, they would have to travel to Detroit and many of them did.

Over the years, I've heard many stories of how much harder life had become for my mom and her siblings, once my grandmother left. The trauma that they had already endured, intensified when Wade realized that my grandmother was not coming back. It's not like he was significantly providing for them anyway. My mother was the youngest out of her siblings that were left with my grandfather in Georgia. Many of those children that *MA'MA* left behind, would eventually find ways to get away from the grips of my grandfather and find their way to Detroit. For example, one of the eldest daughters had moved out and was raising a family of her own in Moultrie and would have nothing to do with my grandfather, three of the boys had joined the army to escape Wade's continuous wrath, one moved to Detroit along with two other sisters, two moved to New Jersey before joining my grandmother in Detroit. Then there were four, my mother, one brother and two sisters, who happened to be the eldest of the children that still lived at home with my grandfather.

Another one of my mother's older sisters was made to work hard in the diner that my grandfather owned. Normally, this would have been one of the many duties that my grandmother had to do, *however*, she'd left him. Now it was up to who my grandfather felt was the next person in line to take her place, that person would be my aunt Mattie Pearl who wasn't that much older than my mother. She would work so hard in that diner from sun up to sun down without any breaks. This forced obligation even prevented her from attending school. The responsibility of making sure the diner stayed opened for the many patrons that frequently came to the spot was just too great. My mother and the other siblings were allowed to go to school but once school was out for the day, they would all have to go directly to the diner and help their sister out. My aunt had grown tired and weary from all of the abuse that she and the other children suffered at the hands of their father. She then decided that the time was nearing for another great escape, like there mother had done some time ago. My aunt began taking and saving a portion of any monies that was made from the diner so that there would be enough funds for her and her siblings to get away. She knew that the money wouldn't be missed because her father trusted that she'd never take it, he'd be too preoccupied with his many obligations to even assume that it was gone.

One could only imagine what was going on in Wade's head to make him this malicious. Even though my grandfather had many occupations and even other women, he still carried hate in his heart for *MA'MA* for leaving him behind. *I mean, the audacity of him to be angry over his wife's leaving him because of the horrible abuse he afflicted upon her and their children is astonishing.* He was truly a confused *yet* broken man, who's abuse continued immensely. There was no reason for me to doubt these accusations or the story for that matter because my mother had plenty of scars to remind her of that faithful life that she once lived. My mother and my aunts often told me of things that happened to them in their adolescent years in Georgia and even though the stories were sad, you could find humor in the way they told them. On one account, I was told by my mother that she would sometimes walk to the local cemetery just to escape the mental and physical abuse of her father. She told me that she would walk into this graveyard where she'd be met by a cave that was deep within the cemetery. As she went through this dark cave, my mother said she'd found a peach tree on the other side. As if she was lead there by spirit to find a sweet moment of peace from an all so bitterly chaotic world. She'd sit under this tree eating peaches without the slightest thought of fear and worry. This tree served as her refuge at a young age and the fruit that it bore, gave her offerings of some of the biggest and sweetest peaches she had ever eaten in her young life. I oftentimes asked her was she ever afraid to go into that cemetery, walk through the cave and sit there amongst the dead and eat those peaches and she told me as sweetly as she could, *"No"*.

My Mother would say to me, *"It's not the dead that you should be afraid of!"* The abuse from my grandfather was so severe, that it caused my mother to put up a mental block in her mind, as if none of those things ever existed...but we knew that they did! I would continuously ask her about the many scars that remained on her body from when she was younger, one scar in particular, she told me she received when both of her parents were fighting. My mother said that she'd got in the way of their altercation and that the result could've left her with a severed foot or potentially ended her life. Wade had pulled out a hatchet during a fight with *MA'MA* and was viciously swinging it at her. While being in this wild rage, he didn't realize who he had struck. When my grandfather snapped out of it, the back of my mother's foot was hanging off. No doctors were called, no police were called in those days out of racial fear and with all the drama that was surrounding this domestic situation, *how could they be called?* Wade, being the backwoods Doctor that he was, had no other choice but to sew the hanging piece of my mother's foot back together, as he was the cause of this brutal incident to begin with. *It's hard to find your soul's true reflection, when your searching through the shattered pieces of life's looking glass...*

The abuse that Wade tormented his children with had become more psychological at this point than physical, he had their minds in constant fear. There would be no more time to waste, they had to go. Keep in mind, that these children had already been in constant escape mode since before *MA'MA* left. There just wasn't enough money or proper planning to run away from this place they'd called home with no adult supervision. All they knew was that there mother had left and was up north, murmurs about her being in Detroit where to be of secret so that Wade's ears wouldn't catch the sound but they still didn't have a clue to where she was exactly. The contemplation of running away was more intense now than it had been over the course of several months, even though the fear of not having enough money for everyone to go was often in their minds. This type of pressure would make even the most mature individual break, one could only imagine how these children stayed strong. Not knowing for certain where they'd go, where their mother was, would they get caught by their father or would something tragic happen to one of them along the way. All of the whelms of fear that any one person could face, they'd faced it head on. Like the hurricanes in the bosom of an Indian Summer, the eye of their storm was passing over and after that storm, the sun began to shine. The day had come where they would leave their father's land behind.

After months of planning, the eldest of my mother's sisters told the second eldest to take the children to school as usual but after school, they were not to come to the diner like they'd normally do. They were to go to the bus station where she'd be anxiously awaiting their arrival. Wade would never be the wiser because she told him that she had to go and get the laundry. The day was perfect for them to leave as he would be making his house calls, delivering medicinal herbs to patrons before arriving at the diner. Not only would he be making medical house calls, Wade would be making other house calls to his many women. This would give them the allotted amount of time to execute their escape perfectly. My aunt picked my mother and the other children up from school, she told them to run as fast as they could to the bus station and to never, ever look back... and they didn't. For that, their bravery and their

selfless act of freedom, I am forever grateful... and because of

that fateful moment in time, here we are.

CHAPTER 2

<u>LIFE AS I KNEW IT:*CONTINUED*</u>

"UNGOWA! I Got That Soul Power!"

{MA'MA yelling from the living room}... "DEBRA ANN!!! TURN THAT MUSIC OFF AND COME AND GET THESE KIDS!"

I can vividly remember my aunt Debra with her big afro, green and yellow flowered bell bottom jumpsuit on, with a black-power fist afro pick sitting neatly in the middle of her hair, eagerly replying, *"Come on y'all! I'm going to teach you guys a routine, so stand right here okay!? Follow my lead as soon as the music starts!"* Aunt Debra immediately ran over to the record player and blew the dust off of the needle, wiped off the album and turned to us and commandingly said,

"You stand right here Kim!" She swiftly moved me into position and directed the other girls too. *"And... You stand here, now everybody raise the peace sign and say Ooh, Ungowa! We got that Soul Power! Ooh Ungowa! We got that Soul Power! (little girl voices, repeating the chant)* *"Now, Kim get down on one knee with your fist in the air and when I tell you, I need you to jump up like this and spin around, okay!"* My aunt continued demonstrating how she wanted us to execute this powerful routine, with excitement and inspiration. *"Everybody ready?" (little girl voices in unison)* *"YES!"* we shouted. Aunt Debra turned the music on and proceeded to do the chant, well that was until I abruptly stopped her and said, *"The only way that this is going to work, is if my hair is like yours. I can't see it no other way!"* Aunt Debra looked at me with attitude and said, *"Really Kim?... Is everybody ready? (silence)... I said is everybody ready?"* Aunt Debra asked again, this time with seriousness. I looked at her with my hands on my hips and said, *"I guess as ready as I'm going to be with my hair looking like this!"* The music began and all I could hear from the record player was harmonic *yet* angelic black

42

voices singing "♪♫ *Young Gifted and Black! That's where it's*

at♪♫!" I twirled and twirled, not knowing if I was doing it

right or not but I made it work. Meanwhile, *MA'MA* placed her

cigarette carefully in the ashtray on the table and shouted, *"Go*

out there and get me a switch off of them bushes cause' I told

them to be QUIET! Damn kids get on my nerves, making all of

that noise. I can't hear shit!" *MA'MA* continued to fuss and

shout, *"Debra, Debra Ann, I thought I told you to keep them*

quiet?" *MA'MA* asked as she re-lit her cigarette, *"I'm not*

playin'! Keep on making all that damn noise hear?! I'm trying

to watch the news. Can y'all please get your kids right now?

My grandmother was overwhelmed and continued to ask her

daughters to come and handle their children, because we were

driving her crazy. *"I can't hear nothing for all that noise and*

turn that damn music off! All of this shit on at the same time.

Ain't nobody paying no bills or giving no money to Mr. Charlie

but me!" *MA'MA* reached her boiling point and sternly yelled,

"FORGET IT!!! I'm going over to Mrs. Williams house to see

if she's heard anything." My grandmother got up off the easy chair with a cigarette hanging from the left side of her lips, looked in my direction and said, *"I'll be back in a minute. Kimberly, don't you take yo black ass outside! Do you hear me talking to you? Don't chu' go outside!"* Before MA'MA could fully step her feet out of the front door to walk around the corner to Mrs. Williams house, *(to get the information on whether the schools would be striking or not)*, my aunt Debra ecstatically shouted *"Mama! Can I go and talk to Gwen and Marianne? I want them to see my knew outfit, and hear this new album I got?"* MA'MA slightly turned around on the front porch, took another drag of her cigarette and said, *"Yes you can.[exhales smoke] Come on, walk with me. I'm on my way to talk to Mrs. Williams right now [inhales more]Come on [exhales smoke]."* My aunt Debra rushed out the door to meet MA'MA on the front porch. I abruptly stopped dancing and ran to the living room and asked, *"Why can't I go outside? It's hot and all of my friends are out there playing. Its just not fair, I can't never do nothing around this stupid place. That's why I hate it here, STUPID!"* I cried, stomping my feet as I walked to the front door of our house.

I looked out the front door and didn't see anyone. I guess it was too hot for them to be out, so I decided to play jacks. I went over to my sister Shay and I asked her to play with me first, *"Can you go outside with me or can you please play jacks with me?"* I begged her, with one hand on my hip and one finger up my nose. *"Get out of my face, you don't even know how to play! Wit yo nasty butt."* Shay replied with attitude, *"Nappy headed thang and you know good and well, Annie (my mom) made us an appointment at May's so we can go get our hair done. That's why you can't go outside."* teased Shay, *"Plus, ain't nobody out there anyway, It's too hot! So stupid, just look at your hair dummy."* As my sister continued to dismiss any notion of playing with me, I continued to stand in front of her with my finger still up my nose, *"So you just gone' stand in my face and keep digging in your nose for gold? I hope you find it."* said Shay with disgust as she continued to tease me, *"I'm going to tell everybody you was digging in your nose, so they won't play with your stupid self and I'm telling on you for saying that you hate something and saying everybody is stupid!"* Shay swiftly pranced by, pushing me out of the way before opening the screen door and letting it slam as she left out. I ran after her as fast as I could, hollering all the while. I didn't even care if she beat me up, I was just that mad. I ran out the front door onto the porch and shouted, *"TELL TELL GO TO JAIL, HANG YOUR BRITCHES ON A NAIL! IF YOU CRY, I'LL PICK THEM UP...IF YOU DON'T, I'LL KICK YOUR BUTT! YO STUPID ASS!"* Shay stopped, turned, looked at me and said *"Say one more thing and I'm going to give your little nasty butt something to really cry for, just keep on Kim!"* I was stopped dead in my tracks, ready for her to come back and punch me but she didn't. Shay did the unthinkable and ran over to my grandmother. *MA'MA* happened to be standing on the corner speaking with Mrs. Williams before my sister abruptly interrupted her to tell on me. *"Kim is outside and she cussin', she said a bad word!"* Shay continued telling and pointing in my direction yelling, *"MA'MA, LOOK! KIM HARDHEADED SELF IS OUTSIDE!"* I was frozen on the porch, I couldn't believe she was telling but most importantly, I couldn't believe that I cussed yet again (*sigh*), *This shit has got to stop!*

{MA'MA to Mrs. Williams}... "This child done brought her black ass outside after I told her (conversation interrupted), wait one minute Mrs. Williams." Annoyed by the way that my sister Shay disrupted her conversation with Mrs. Williams and mad that I didn't obey her, *MA'MA* turned towards my direction and yelled, *"KIMBERLY! DIDN'T I TELL YOU NOT TO BRING YOUR NARROW ASS OUTSIDE? GO IN THE HOUSE RIGHT NOW!"* After my grandmother cursed me out, I turned to walk back in the house but was halted when I heard my sister Shay say, *"That's what your stupid butt gets and for your information, you didn't even say the words right dummy!"* Shay stood there with a yellow halter top with yellow and white shorts on, white flowered sandals and a big bushy ponytail rolling her eyes and neck while sticking her tongue out at me before running down the street. I looked at her and screamed *"SO WHAT! That's why I'm telling on you for punching me in my legs all the time, you DUMMY ASS SHIT!"* I quickly slammed the screen door behind me, plopped down in front of the stairs where the baby pigs lived near our front door and hollered, *"I DON'T CARE ANYWAY!"* After I'd calmed

down a bit, I had begun playing jacks by myself. I'd got to my sixes when the ball suddenly got away from me and rolled down the hole in front of the steps. While in the process of reaching for it, I quickly stopped when I heard my mother's voice. She, along with her cousin Barbara, best friend Frenchy and a few other cousins were speaking about my dad. I had to hear what they were talking about, so I got up and went over to my mom and sat on her lap while she was in mid conversation. *"Yeah girl, he's supposed to come over and bring me the money to go get them some school clothes and get their hair done cause' I ain't about to tussle with them girls and all that hair. Specially this one!"* She stated as I pretended to be sad while I was on her lap but in reality, I was only trying to listen to their conversation. The chatter seemed continuous until my mom asked if they'd heard about something...*"You know the rabbit died, right?"* My mom asked, looking and awaiting a response from her friends. She was almost desperate for their reaction to what she'd just laid on them. *"Ooh girl, I knew it!"* shouted Barbara with excitement *"Because I sho' have been dreaming of fish"* she stated, *"I'm glad it's not me girl, you better keep*

48

that man away from you! Did you tell him? (slight pause) Girl,

how you gone tell Mattie Lee?" asked Barbara, in fear of how

my grandmother would react, (*to whatever it was my mom was*

speaking of) . While she stared at my mother with concern, I

had to find out what they were really *gossiping* about.

"Mommy, what rabbit died? Who killed it? I asked with even

greater concern. *"Yo daddy killed it!"* shouted Frenchy

humorously, triggering laughter from everyone. As everyone

continued laughing, I continued on with my investigation.

"That's why I never liked that man and his mama looks like

Charlie Brown!" They all continued to laugh even harder but I

was dead serious. My mother looked at me, slid me off of her

lap, patted me on the behind and said, *"Get your little tail out*

of here, go on!" Before I could fully walk away, I had to hear

what my mom was concluding ... *"Yes girl, I told him! Now, I*

just have to break it to mama. You know John don't care about

*having no babies, the more the merrier to him. "*As my mom

carried on with her explanation (*of whatever news she was*

breaking to her friends), I pretended that I left something but

my mom knew very well what I was doing, *"Kimberly! Didn't*

I tell you to get out of here?" She entreated while being in mid conversation. I looked at her and said, *"Oh yeah, I forgot my ball. Don't forget to tell that man, my daddy, that if he is going to be killing rabbits, we don't want him near us... & Especially, you don't want him near us at all cause' what if he tried to kill us? & You don't want to see him either, okay mommy?"* After my valid speech about whether my father should be allowed around us, I gave my mother a big hug and ran to get a flashlight out of the kitchen drawer. Once I returned with the flashlight, it was my duty to retrieve my ball from the hole in front of the steps that it rolled down into. I got down on my knees, pointed the flashlight down the hole, turned it on and there they were, the little baby pigs were sleeping peacefully. Once I spotted my orange ball, I extended my arm as far as I could down the hole. I had to move the baby pigs out of the way of my ball and I surely didn't want to wake them up. Just as I was inches away from grabbing my ball, I heard someone screaming my name (*Kimberly*). It was my mother, running with a powder blue mini dress on, with a white wing collar and her big Afro swiftly swaying from how quickly she was

50

moving in her wedge heel sandals towards me... *"KIMBERLY!*

Don't put your hand down there! Those things might bite you!"

she shouted, right before quickly grabbing me up by my arm.

"I'll be right back y'all and if John comes, tell him to give me

a minute!" My mom looked at me and ushered me off to the

bathroom, washing my hands and arms very hard. *"(water*

running from the sink) Mommy, why that man comin' over

here" I cried, while my mother continued to wash me...

"OUCH! You're hurting me. All I wanted to do was get my

ball, those pigs never bite me! Now tell me, why is he coming

over? Cause' if you don't, I'm telling MA'MA!" I continued

whining as my mom grabbed a towel to dry my hands and arms

off, she then began thoroughly checking to see if I had any bite

marks and scratches. *"Annie Ruth, John here! Did you here*

me? J.B is here!" yelled Frenchy from the bottom of the stairs,

in attempt to alert my mom of my dads arrival. *"Now go get me*

that comb and brush... and don't forget the grease!" stated my

mom rushingly, while she ushered me along. I looked at her

with a frown on my face, tears whaling up in my eyes and

screamed, *"WHY? I DID'T SAY I WANTED MY HAIR*

COMBED, YOU JUST DOING THAT CAUSE' HE'S HERE! &

WHY SHOULD I? AREN'T WE GOING TO MAY'S? YOU

ALWAYS DO THIS TO ME" I cried, *"YOU'RE ONLY DOING*

THIS CAUSE' HE KILLED ALL OF THOSE BUNNIES, I'M

TELLING MA'MA!" My mother looked at me and said, *"So,*

you want your daddy to see your hair looking like this?" I

folded my arms and said, *"I really don't care!"* My mother

stared at me with slight disappointment and said, *"Now*

Kimberly, don't act mean like that! Don't you want to look

pretty when you go outside to play and when you go to

school?" I answered her with a quick response saying, *"Yes,*

when I go outside but it ain't gone be no school never! I hope

you know and any old way, MA'MA told me I couldn't go out,

so what's the use of you combing my hair or me getting it

done? I'm never going to do it! I hope you know, I'm telling

too, that he killed those animals!" I hurriedly stomped out of

the room but was stopped by what my mother was saying.

"Well, go ahead and go outside and play but remember you're

the one who wanted the Shirley Temple Curls" she said as my

mood began to change, & *"When I call your butt in the house, you have to promise to let me comb your hair before I take you girls around to May's and you better not open your mouth and say a God damn thing to my mama! Do you hear me talking to you Kimberly?"* My Mother's voice shifted from soft and sweet to stern in an instant, I knew she was serious about me not mentioning anything to *MA'MA*. I looked at her with my arms folded and replied, *"Okay, it's a deal!"* Hell, that's all I wanted to do in the first place, go outside.

As I started to run off with excitement, I was halted *yet* again, *"Before you go out that door little girl, come and give your daddy a hug and a kiss?"* stated my dad as I was in pursuit down the steps. I looked at him thinking to myself, *"I wish the hell I would! Who does he think I am? My mama?"* He then picked me up and gave me a big wet kiss on the cheek, I kept my arms folded and my legs straight the whole time. My dad could only laugh as he placed me back down on the floor but I was just glad to finally be able to exit out the front door. I was now able to greet the outside world but I could still hear their loud conversation and my mom saying to her friends, *"That Kimberly is something else. I hope she don't tell Mama nothing*

53

cause' I don't want to hear her mouth." She said, *"John, you know your daughter put her hands down there with those rats? Talking about, they are baby pigs. Mama has got to get someone out here to put that poison down to kill those rats! They're getting to be really bad, especially when my little baby calling them pigs, poor thing!"* My mom and her friends continued to laugh and gossip while listening to music loudly on the radio. My dad then pulled my mother closer and said, *"I told you to get yawl stuff and come live with me"* My mother stared at him and said, *"I might as well stay here with my mother! Why would I leave here, to live with your mother? That makes no sense John!"* Dad, being a boastful hustler, reached into his pocket, pulled out a wad of money and handed it to my mother. I wiped my face off with my hand as hard as could from that stupid kiss, I jumped off the porch, thinking to myself, *"I guess she rich now!"* but I didn't want to hear anymore of that nonsense they were talking. I was not about to live with no murderer, so I ran as fast as I could. I was trying to get as far away from the house as possible, I couldn't let my grandmother see that I had come outside. Despite the fact that my mother said I could go out, *MA'MA* was the boss of that house and everyone in it and since she initially said that I couldn't go outside, I knew that if she caught me I'd be in a lot of trouble. My grandmother was the type that *meant what she said* and *said what she meant*, this was definitely one of those moments that she meant for me not to go outside.

I took off running down the street, in hopes of not being spotted by *MA'MA*. I ran over to my friend Bun's house who happened to live at the other end of the block, so that we could gather all of our friends together. I had to ask them all a very important question and I knew that he would know where everyone was. As everyone gathered around, I began speaking and posed my question. *"Did you guys know that the schools are supposed to be on strike?"* They all looked at me with a sense of bewilderment on their dirty, sticky faces. I paced back and forth with my finger tapping my chin, stopping in front of each of them. One at a time, I began looking them dead in their eyes. I knew that they didn't know, plus I was the one with all

of the brains. *"It's apparent that you don't know what that means."* I stated while pacing, *"Okay, my mom always tells us what stuff means or look it up in a dictionary. Y'all are so dumb!"* I continued my slight dictatorship with my hands on my hips, *"Anyway, It means that we may not have to ever go back to school because they need some money, I guess. Anyway, I asked a question. Do y'all like school?"* I looked around at their dirty chubby faces for a reply but there was a slight pause or silence that fell over them. My friend Michael caught my attention as he stood there eating a popsicle, that had dripped down his dirty hands. *"You are so disgusting Michael, that's just nasty, and why didn't you get your momma to give us all a popsicle? You are so inconsideration and nasty. I promise to God you are!"* I shouted but before I could gather my thoughts, out of nowhere I hear a little voice say, *"What that mean Kim, inconsideration? & Sometimes, I do."* I looked and screamed with my fist balled up ready to strike the culprit, *"Who said that? I said, what dummy said that?* I sinisterly whispered with a mean face, daring one of them to speak up...
"I DID!" replied Bun gleefully, *"Well, well! So, you like*

56

school?" I asked while slowing approaching him. As I got closer to Bun, I balled my fist up and punched him in the stomach before sternly saying, *"Then your ass don't belong here with any of us. All in favor of this dummy leaving and never ever being allowed in our club, say I because I have something to tell y'all and he is no longer my friend."* I'd declared Bun an outcast and continued on, *"I'm going to tell y'all in your ear, of course, so he can't hear us!"* Bun stood there bent over holding his stomach while I walked around, whispering in everyone's ears saying, *"Act like I said something funny and laugh! (children laughing)"*. After telling everyone to laugh, I looked at Bun and said, *"Well dummy, I guess your time is up here because we don't talk to traitors. Everyone in favor of Bun not being here, say I!"* Everyone raised their hand and shouted *"I"* in unison. I looked at him and commandingly said, *"Well well well. Bun Honey, the I's have it. So, it's time that you leave. Go home Bun and don't never come back!"* Before Bun could fully accept or grasp the mutiny that I'd cast upon him, I punched him in the stomach one more time. Bun doubled over letting out a loud scream. His nose started running and he began to cry, dragging his bike down the street. Before he could fade into the distance, I chased after him. It wasn't because I was sorry but because *MA'MA* was down there and I knew that he would tell on me. So, as not to get into any trouble with my grandmother for being outside and hitting Bun, I allowed him to come back. I'd lifted his banishment and yelled, *"Bun... Bun... Bun, don't cry baby! I was just playing, I psyched your mind! Psych' your mind, your booty shine, I heard it on channel nine."* I nervously sang as everyone began laughing, welcoming Bun back into our group. *"Now stop all that crying sweet baby! You are a big boy right? If you keep crying, I'm going to make you go home for real and I'm not going to be your friend. Now give me a hug sweet baby! Come on, give me a hug!"* I pulled Bun closer for a hug and ordered everyone else to apologize to him, *"Now everybody, give Bun a hug, cause' he's sad and yawl made him sad, cause' y'all wanted him to leave and if it wasn't for me, he would be home all alone crying cause of yawl."* I'd cunningly placed the blame onto everyone else, all while eyeing my friend Tanya's Big Wheel. *"Now Bun, you know I'm your best friend? The only one you got and well I guess, we are*

all friends again. If we are and you really believe in your heart

to God that we are, give me a big hug and a push down the

street!" After Bun forgave me and agreed to give me a push on

a big wheel that I hadn't even acquired, it was time to tell

them all what I had planned. *"GET OFF OF THAT BIG*

WHEEL TANYA! DID YOU HEAR ME? I shouted, *"Give me*

your Big Wheel, before I take it and keep it! Now, everyone

who wants to hear my idea follow me!" I screamed, as I rode

Tanya's *Big Wheel* as fast as I could down the street. Everyone

who did not have a bike, or anything to ride, ran after me.

After we all flew down the street, followed by the scorching

Sun, we finally made it to the end of the block. I hopped off of

the *Big Wheel* that my friend Tanya, so willingly gave me and

presented what I had up my sleeves. *"Okay, so a lot of you*

never mentioned if you liked school or not except for Bun...

Bun you're so brave." I walked around everyone with my

hands hidden before showing them the pack of matches that I'd been secretly holding onto in my pocket. *"I need all of you to stand in a line and one by one, I am going to whisper in your ear and tell you what I am planning on doing! Then, I am going to let you touch the matches. Then we have to cut our fingers and put our blood together like they did on television in that one movie, so I can know you're not going to tell and..."* I had them wrapped around my fingers, they didn't have a clue of what I was about to say next. *"You are going to do what I ask! If you want, you can stay, that is if you like my idea or go home forever if you don't like it after I tell you."* I whispered in their ears one by one and everyone looked to be so afraid, but no one left. *"Since none of you left, that means you are all interested in my plan!"* They all looked at me and said, *"Why you talk like that?"* I looked back at them and replied, *"Talk like what?"* Bun looked at me and said, *"One of those white girls on the tv!"* I rubbed my hands together with a sinister look on my face, stuck my sticky hands in my pocket and grabbed the matches. *"IF YOU DON'T SHUT THE HELL UP RIGHT NOW BUN, I AM GOING TO SET YOU ON FIRE!*

WATCH AND SEE WHAT I TELL YOU, CAUSE' I REALLY

DON'T CARE!" I'd threateningly shouted at Bun, daring him

to make one more sound. *"Now, if Bun is finished cracking*

jokes about me, I would ask that everybody please gather

around!" They all slowly gathered closer to each other, *"Ooh,*

yawl so stupid! I mean gather around me, please!" I yelled ,

"Since none of us and I do mean none of us, really like school,

I am going to blow up the world and that way we don't ever

have to go to school, forever!" I'd ecstatically revealed my

sinister plan, *"Everybody, say forever! Forever!"* As my

friends rallied around me chanting the word *Forever*, I kicked

out the basement window on the side of the house and struck

each and every match that I could gather and find but... nothing

happened *(the chants stop)...."Hey Kimmy, why isn't the world*

blowing up?" They'd all asked with confusion written all over

their faces, *"Yeah, why didn't the world blow up yet? You're a*

liar! Let's go y'all!" Shouted Bun with disappointment, as

everyone else followed. *"Yeah let's go, cause' she gone be in*

big trouble!" They all walked away hollering, while I was left

deserted. I had lost control of the situation but needed to regain their trust, *"Wait a minute, it just takes time that's all."* I'd shouted as they got further away, *"You'll see, when we don't have to go to school ever again."* I stated with assurance but they just kept walking, *"So, you guys are just going to leave like that? Well I don't care and you better not tell on me Bun!"* I screamed as they continued on their merry way, I was left abandoned with an empty matchbox. The angels had to have been watching over me that day, I could have killed many souls. Thank the Lord that didn't happen, I should've stayed in the house.

CHAPTER 3

REMINISCE

"Children of the Revolution"

{Marvin Gaye's "Trouble Man" begins playing on the radio}

... "DEATH TO RICHARD NIXON! (children marching and repeating the chant) DEATH TO FASCIST BABYLON! (children continue to march and repeat the chant) I SAY RIGHT ON, I SAY RIGHT ON, RIGHT ON, RIGHT ON, RIGHT ON!" (chant begins to echo/fade with ambience)...

As I close my eyes and drift back to a particular place in time during my childhood, I'm reminded that things seemed more authentic. From the people, the places and things that gave me the vantage point to my culture's raw imagery, I can honestly say I had no worries. Every angle of my five senses, points me towards the direction of what makes nostalgia bittersweet at times. I can see the vision clearly, I can hear it's sound vividly as *Mr. Softies* ice cream truck rides slowly down our street. I can also smell it's aroma in the air and my tongue can very well taste the foods of the time of my childhood. Sometimes, all it takes is a catchphrase, an image, a song, someone or something along those lines, to spark the brittle wit of nostalgia; even though over time, it may become harder to reignite. Traveling back in my mind, I can see the unrest and uneasiness that was reaching its zenith during those times as well. I grew up in a post civil rights era that educed the minds of political revolutionaries, activists, social movements and a black power *mixtape* that quintessentially shifted the dynamics of my culture. It was normal for revolutionaries to oppose the corrupt system that we as people suffered under. Before you begin to wonder why someone would be marching for the death of the 37th president, you should know that there is no secret that this great country of the United States of America, has had its share of turbulence when it comes to the racial spectrum. Especially, when it pertains to the advancement of my people in this country. America has always feared or dreaded the day that we'd fight back, *I can understand why*. For starters, our misrepresented beginning in this hemisphere of the earth has been a very trying one. We've been stolen, misplaced, misnamed, mistreated, sold, beaten and lynched in a very familiar *yet* strange land. When the days of slavery ended, our people suffered some of the most difficult conditions that any human being could've suffered but some how survived. They survived a false reconstruction, a war of *their* worlds and migrated to the north, east and west to establish prominence. Though many of those prominent towns were bulldozed, burned down and their ashes blown across the nation, throughout the wind's midst were the seeded sparks of revolution that would engulf many movements of black power.

One in particular that I recall, was the BPP *(Black Panther Party)*. Though it's inception had its difficulties, their revolutionary approach toward combating an unjust system would give hope as well as breathe new life into a hopeless people. Throughout the nation, there would be a BPP chapter within the black community of that particular city and I was fortunate enough to live in a city like Detroit, that had one. I remember some of the leaders in our community riding down our street with a fresh produce truck to pass out fruits and vegetables, they even had a book mobile that came to pass out books to the people. I remember me and my sisters participating in many of those different programs that they implemented from a 10 point perspective of organizing. I can vividly recall a day when we were given breakfast and lunch from their *Free Breakfast* program. It seemed like mountains of children would be lined up in the school cafeteria, awaiting there meals. Standing in line with my older sisters and some of there friends from our neighborhood, gave me a birds eye view of what was happening in our community, though the visual seemed blurred for others. After we'd eat breakfast, the revolutionaries would have a bagged lunch for us. Even though I dreaded eating the bologna sandwiches they'd offered, I thought what was being done by these militants was powerful. Strangely, that very powerful program was considered a major threat to the government. *How could feeding children, some who hadn't ate a meal in days, be of any threat to old white men in government?* I mean, they were in such fear of little black boys and girls in the ghetto being fed, mentally and physically that they made it top priority to eliminate, terminate and compromise this organization. I remember sitting there in the cafeteria and the militants would be very positive and encouraging to the youth, *hell*, even the white people who worked for the school, seemed to enjoy when we would sing *Motown* songs or *Negro Spirituals. So, where was the threat in that? I guess Hoover had the answers to the equation.*

"... The Black Panther Party's Free Breakfast program is the greatest threat to efforts by authorities to neutralize the BPP and destroy what it stands for."- J. Edgar Hoover

A DAY WITH MRS. FREEMAN

I opened my eyes, peeked through the window and was instantly captivated by images of black excellence, when I spotted my sisters and cousins marching in formation with the neighborhood's avid revolutionary. I still could hear Marvin Gaye's *"Trouble Man"* playing on the radio near where the Smith's lived. It was just something so mesmerizing about the way they marched with pride, joy and syncopation to Marvin's music, as if they knew their place in this world. [*marching continues*]...*"Death to Richard Nixon, death to Richard Nixon, death to fascist Babylon, death to fascist Babylon, I say right on, I say right on, right on, right on, right on."* As my family marched on with the militant, I had to make my way over to where they were. It didn't matter to me that they were screaming for the death of the 37th president, *it's not like his tricky ass was my friend or something.* I had to be apart of what was happening, so I went for it. I excitedly ran outside, didn't look both ways before crossing the street, with my fist pumping in the air yelling, *"CAN I DO IT TOO? I WANT TO DO IT! DEATH TO RICHARD NIXON!"* I'd passionately shouted with high enthusiasm. I was ready to be welcomed into their revolutionary march with open arms, given a black leather coat with a matching beret and black shades to cover my eyes from *"THE MAN"* but (*sigh*), I was quickly shot down by the piercing words of my older sister. *"GO HOME KIM! RIGHT NOW OR I'M TELLING ON YOU!"* She yelled forcefully, without missing a beat. I quickly ran back across the street to avoid getting in trouble, *so much for the revolution*. With my activist days behind me, I decided to go in the house to watch tv. *What did I decide to turn on, you ask? THE BRADY BUNCH, OKAY!!! Don't judge me!* I'd done this on so many occasions *yet* this time seemed oddly different. My mom happened to be working for the *Numbers Man* at the end of the block and hadn't made it home *yet*, so food wasn't prepared. I was very hungry, so I decided to go into the kitchen where *MA'MA* was sitting, smoking a cigarette as usual and said,

"I'm hungry!" My grandmother looked at me with a stern look on her face and replied, *"Eat some cereal until Annie Ruth comes home, then she will get dinner ready"* I couldn't wait that long, so I stared her down with tears forming in my eyes and said, *"I really want some rice and gravy!"* I cried. *"OH HELL NO!"* shouted *MA'MA*, *"You ain't getting no rice and gravy, cause' we ain't got none cooked! Now gone and eat some cereal until yo mama get home!"* She yelled, taking another drag of her cigarette. *"Okay but you know there is no milk here for no cereal, MA'MA!"* I cried. My grandmother looked at me, took another long drag of her cigarette, blew rings of smoke out of here half parched lips and said, *"Wait until your mama gets home then, now gone and get out of here! [blows smoke]Did you here me? Right now and don't go outside!"* After being dismissed by *MA'MA* and her cloud of smoke, something told me to wait around a bit before fully walking away *[door closes]*. I suddenly heard the back screen door slam shut, I knew right then and there that *MA'MA* had left. I kinda figured that she would eventually go over to Mrs. Williams house to talk about nothing sooner or later, now was

70

my chance to live a little. I peeked around every corner in the house, trying to see what I could get away with but there was nothing to do. After mischievously casing our house a few times, I snuck out the front door. I stood there anxiously excited, glad to finally be out of the house but that feeling quickly changed when I noticed no one was out there except our neighbor Mrs. Freeman. I began looking in all directions, seeing if I could spot any of my friends but to no avail, just Mrs. Freeman sitting eerily quiet on her front porch with a beer in her hand. Before I could make any sudden movement, Mrs. Freeman turned in my direction and said, *"If you're lookin' for the ice cream truck, it ain't out her [sips beer]. Come here little girl! Did you here me? Come here right now!"* I turned around, looking to see if anyone noticed her sitting there with that beer in her hand but there still wasn't anybody out. I believe she might've been drunk or as my grandmother would say *"Having one of her spells"* again. *What was one of her spells, you ask?* Well, Mrs. Helen Freeman happened to be a Schizophrenic who suffered through bouts of mental illness. However, back in those days mental health wasn't of major concern in our neighborhood or their wasn't any way to successfully treat it outside of heavy medication and not to mention, they just called it a spell. *"Come here, I got some cookies."* She slurred. I began to walk slowly over to her house, looking over my shoulder to see if anyone was paying attention but to my surprise, no one was looking out. It wasn't odd that she was calling me over, I had been inside her place several times before but only with my grandmother. As I was walking to her house, I put my hand on my hip and said sarcastically, *"I wasn't lookin' for the ice cream truck, now where is the cookies?"* She looked at me and laughed sinisterly, *"Come on in, you want some?"* stated Mrs. Freeman, extending her hand to offer me a swig from the can of beer she was holding. I swiftly shook my head from side to side, with my hands on my hips, rolling my neck and with a catty tone replied, *"No thank you, my mama don't let me drink that stuff. Anyway, I thought you said you had some cookies?"* Mrs. Freeman, puzzled by my response, stared at me like she was dazed and said, *"I do, with your smart ass. Come over here and sit down and eat these cookies! Since you don't want none of this [lifts beer can, slightly shaking it], do you want some milk?"* I looked at her while placing a cookie in my mouth and sarcastically said, *"I don't like milk unless it's in a bowl of cereal! You still got that horse in that room? If you do, can I ride it?"* I'd asked, before swindling my way into more cookies. *"Oh, by the way, I'm going to need some more of those cookies!"* Mrs. Freeman looked at me with a crazed stare in her eyes, then gently said *"I moved it upstairs, so Kilroy can ride it."* I was a bit puzzled by what she said but still too young to recognize the signs of her having one of those *spells*. I looked at her and said, *"Your son Kilroy? He's a grown man and he still rides this horse?"* I'd asked, while running up the stairs in pursuit of the room she'd hid the horse in. Once I discovered the horse, Mrs. Freeman allowed me to ride it freely liked she'd done many times before. I was ecstatic to be able to do what I wanted to do but again, something wasn't quite right and I started to sense it. After riding and being on that horse, for what seemed to me like hours, I tried to finally get off. However, Mrs. Freeman would not allow me to. She just stared at me and yelled, *"Stay your ass on that horse! That's what you wanted and you need to win this race! NOW RIDE FASTER!"* Mrs. Freeman

screamed, triggering me to cry. *"I need to go home Mrs. Helen,*

cause' MA'MA told me not to leave out of the house!" I cried,

begging her to let me leave but she wouldn't. She just

frighteningly stared at me and yelled, *"You're not going*

anywhere! Now shut up and keep riding that horse, cause' your

almost there!" I continued riding, crying and exhausted from

being on there for so long but I stayed on. I was very afraid and

didn't know what would happen to me. Suddenly, I heard a

door close and instantly thought that I was going to be set free

but I wasn't. It was Mr. Freeman and he was just as clueless or

as bad as she was. I knew he wouldn't let me leave either, so I

devised a plan to make my escape. I looked at the Freeman's

and frantically said, *"I have to use the bathroom, can I please*

go?" I cried continuously but they weren't phased by my plea.

Mrs. Freeman just looked at me and shouted once more, *"Why*

you have to go the bathroom? You didn't drink anything, pee in

them diapers!" Mrs. Freeman had begun to laugh

uncontrollably loud and the more she laughed, the more I cried.

I was so afraid and thought I was done for, until I heard a loud knock at their front door. It was my aunt Sarah, who we all called Shaky, coming to my rescue. Mrs. Freeman opened the door half way and my aunt demanded to see me, *"Where is Lemma? (one of my many nicknames) Mrs. Smith said she seen you call for her to come over."* Mrs. Freeman stared my aunt down and shouted, *"Well, she ain't here and tell Mrs. Smith I said, MIND HER OWN DAMN BUSINESS!"* Mrs. Freeman then tried to slam the door on my aunt but Shaky pushed the door as hard as she could, knocking Mrs. Freeman out of the way. My aunt forcefully made her way into the house, hollering out my name, *"Lemma, Lemma are you here?"* she yelled, as I cried out from the top of the stairs. *"She won't let me out! She told me that I could never go home. I'm so scared!"* I quickly ran down the stairs, where I was retrieved by my aunt. Shaky hugged me and said, *"Go home and let me deal with this crazy bitch!"* She shoved me out of their front door and I ran as fast as I could. I looked back at my aunt as she had her finger in Mrs. Helen Freeman's forehead saying, *"Listen here you crazy drunk, if I ever here tell of you keeping my niece against her will, matter of fact, you can't ever have her over to your house again! I will kill your crazy ass!"* She shouted before scolding Mr. Freeman *"AND YOUR STUPID ASS!"* she shouted *"YOU'RE HER HUSBAND, YOU SHOULD HAVE KNOWN BETTER!"* Shaky pushed Mrs. Freeman so hard, that she stumbled back into a chair as her husband stood there, idly dumbfounded by the drama that was unfolding. As my aunt left the Freeman's house and came back, I felt a sense of relief as I stood in the doorway. Well, that little moment of peace would abruptly be cut short, as all I could hear coming from my grandmother's mouth was *"Go and get a switch off of that bush, cause' if you wouldn't have taken your bad ass outside, then none of this would have ever happened!"* Needless to say, I got *yet* another ass whipping. I knew there would be plenty more whippings to come, so I decided to run and hide.

My mother finally came home from work and was brought up to speed of the events that took place from her younger sister but I was nowhere to be found. *"Where did she go? Where is my baby? Kimberly, where are you?"* My mother shouted with concern, looking for me throughout the house. I hid in the bathroom upstairs after I got whooped and removed the diamond doorknobs from the door. My mom slowly walked up the stairs with my cousin following behind her saying, *"Kimberly, where are you?"* I could only think to myself that I was going to run far away from that place, *"I'm going to run away to California, so I can meet Michael Jackson and have a thousand dollars after I sell these diamonds"* I stated to myself, after removing the doorknobs. My young mind thought, those clear doorknobs were diamonds and would net me lots of money. I could here my mom approaching the bathroom door, so I decided to climb the wall. She then peeked through the hole where the doorknobs were supposed to be and seen me holding onto the towel rack, steadily climbing up but that didn't stop her from still calling out for me. I walked along the bathtub, holding onto the shower curtains while still ignoring my mother. I could hear my cousin in the background, trying to explain to my mother what she thought happened and what could be of possibility to my whereabouts. *"Maybe she ran away to join the circus or maybe she climbed out the window!"* stated my cousin but my mom knew that was just

children's talk. She turned and looked at my cousin and said,

"Go and get me a butter knife sweetie. Can you do that, so that

I can get Kimberly out of the bathroom? She's just a little mad

right now and I need to talk with her. Can you do that for me?"

My cousin replied by asking, *"Is Lemma going to be alright?"*

My mom assured her that everything would be alright, *"Yes,*

she'll be fine." After my cousin returned with the butter knife,

my mother rescued me. She'd saved me from the bathroom,

from myself, made me a nice tuna sandwich and I was alright.

MICHAEL AND THE SHEPHERD DOG

The next day came and it was like the issues of yesterday never existed in my life. I quickly jumped out of bed, anxiously awaiting the news on whether we had to go to school or not, because that was the buzz around the house. I washed up, put on my clothes, went into the kitchen and eagerly asked those four magic words, *"Can I Go Outside?"* My mom was on her way out of the house to go to work and before she could even give me her blessing to leave the house, *MA'MA* looked at me and sternly said *"No, you cannot!"* I turned around angrily stomping my feet, exclaiming *"Why not? I never get to go outside. Everybody else gets a chance to go out and play except me, why can't I ever go outside?"* I shouted while crying. My grandmother grabbed me by the arm, spanked me on my butt and while in mid swing she stated, *"Because I said so, that's why! Now go and sit your narrow behind down, before I really give you something to cry about."* After I got whooped *yet* again, I ran through the house, sat on the stairs near where the baby pigs lived and started crying. I was overwhelmed with disappointment, until I heard *MA'MA* get up and come towards where I was sitting. *"Remember what I said Kimberly, don't you go outside! You know someone has to watch you cause' you too clumsy, you might get hurt. Now gone and wash your face! Then come sit right here until I get back in the house and then maybe, I'll let you go outside for a little while. I have to go and talk to Mrs. Williams about something."* My grandmother lit her cigarette and exited the front door. She stood on the corner near the bushes, waiving at Mrs. Smith who walked across the street to join the conversation. The three of them stood there talking and laughing, I couldn't help but look out the front door. *"She always talkin' to Mrs. Stupid Smith and Mrs. Williams and she's not gonna ever stop talking or come back to let me go outside."* I shouted, while heading to the backdoor. Now was my chance to make an escape. It didn't matter that my grandmother said she might let me go outside, I wanted to go out there now. *"Why should they have all the fun, while I'm stuck in this stupid house!"* I screamed, releasing all of my disappointment. I jumped up, wiped the tears from my eyes, grabbed my bike and went out the back. I'd pushed my bike three houses over and knocked on Mrs. Williams backdoor, to see if my friend Michael *(her grandson)* could come outside with me. The door opened and Michael's mother Gwen was standing there. *"Can Michael come out and play?"* I asked. She looked at me with some reservation and said, *"I thought your grandmother said you couldn't come out to play today because of what you did yesterday? Sounds like you're on a punishment to me Kim."* Michael's mom then handed me a cookie while I tried to explain, *"No, I'm not! She changed her mind. She said I could come out, get Michael and take him for a ride on my bike. Now can he come or not?"* I'd asked her once more, with one hand on my bike and the other on my hip, as she offered me a glass of *Kool-Aid.* *"Yeah, I guess he can go. Michael, Kim is here for you!"* She shouted, *"Go on out on the back porch! While I go and ask Mrs. Wade did she tell Kim*

81

she could come outside and over here for that matter." I sensed

Gwen would go looking to see if she spotted *MA'MA* and she

did. When she looked out the door to gesture for my

grandmother, I pulled Michael closer and aggressively said *"Yo*

stupid mama make me sick! She is going to tell my grandma on

me, so If you want to ride on my bike you better hurry up and

come on! Right now Michael!" I screamed, hurrying off the

porch and causing my bike to fall down the steps, while the

pedals scraped my legs. I couldn't hold it, there were way too

many stairs on that porch. With my legs burning and scratched

up, I then rushingly grabbed my bike up from the ground,

jumped on it and turned to Michael and asked, *"Are you*

coming or what?" He paused for a moment with a bewildering

look on his face and said, *"I thought your grandma said you*

couldn't!" Before Michael could finish his sentence, I shouted

"GET ON THIS DAMN BIKE MICHAEL!" Michael hurried to

get on the back of my bike, *"I didn't say get on the back. NO*

WAY! Get your black ass on the handlebars!" I yelled, as

Michael jumped off the back seat and ran around to my

handlebars. Once he got on, I took off down the street. No

grass, dirt, gravel or bumps could stop me from getting away from the wrath that *MA'MA* would afflict upon me if she knew that I defied her orders. Michael and I rode around the corner and came back at the other end of our block. We approached Mrs. LeShea's house with caution, this was due to us both being aware of the German Shepherd that she owned. As we passed by the front door of the house, Michael suddenly started screaming *"HELP!"* Mrs. LeShea's dog had gotten loose and began to chase after us. In a panic, I began to scream out for help as well. *"MAMA, HELP ME PLEASE!"* I cried but that didn't stop the German Shepherd from gaining on us. *"GET OFF OF MY BIKE MICHAEL! No sense in both of us getting eaten!"* I screamed while Michael was holding on for dear life to my handlebars. As the German Shepherd continued to gain momentum, I did the unthinkable and sacrificed Michael. I pushed him off my handlebars and began riding my bike as fast as possible, he was holding me back. I was riding my bike so fast, that one training wheel was up in the air but that didn't slow me down. I turned to look over my shoulder to make sure the dog wasn't coming, my bike started wiggling uncontrollably but what I saw can never be erased from my mind. Mrs. LeShea's German Shepherd had captured Michael and had him pent to the ground. I quickly turned around, continuing to ride my bike as fast as possible. I didn't want to get in trouble and most importantly, I didn't want to get a whipping from *MA'MA* for disobeying her by being outside when she specifically told me not too. When I got home, I ran around to the back of the house, put my bike on the porch and walked out the front door as if nothing had ever happened.

"KIMBERLY!!! Didn't I tell you not to come outside? Gwen told me that you came over for Michael, after I told you not to take your ass outside!" yelled *MA'MA*. I fearfully looked at her with tears in my eyes and said, *"I didn't go to see Michael at all MA'MA, she telling a story on me!"* I cried, *"But, but... but I did see Michael running down the street when I was looking out the front door and he was running from Kitty's and nem' dog and MA'MA, I think that dog got Michael!"* MA'MA looked at me with fear in her eyes and said, *"What did you say?"* With my head down and my voice very low, I replied *"I said, I think that German Shepherd dog got Michael and he*

probably ate him up by now!" MA'MA hurried out the door.

She, along with Mrs. Smith and Mrs. Williams started running

down the street in pursuit to save what was left of Michael.

"I'm going to beat your ass when I get back, cause' I told you

not to come outside!" shouted MA'MA as she and Mrs.

Williams continued to run down the street. I knew I was in big

trouble but before I could make a run for it, I heard my mother

coming towards me. She was just coming in from work and

didn't have a clue to what was going on. *"Hi Remily (one of my*

many nicknames), where is Mama?" She asked with concern,

as she looked through the mail on the table. *"Well, (slight*

pause)Her and Mrs. Williams grabbed bats and ran down the

street to get Michael!" I quickly explained. My mom looked at

me with shock and said *"Why? Where is Michael and what's*

going on?" My mother couldn't believe what she was hearing

from me, so I looked at her and said *"I don't know but I think*

Mrs. Kitty's dog got him!" My mother could see straight

through me, she knew I wasn't telling her the whole story.

"What? What do you mean Kitty's dog has Michael, you know

what? I know that you had something to do with this and I am

85

going to beat your butt when I get back." She stated sternly, "Do you hear me talking to you Kimberly? Got my mama and her elderly friends out there trying to save Michael. Whose going to save them!? I'm going to whoop you!" My mother grabbed a big stick and ran after the grandmothers, in hopes of saving and rescuing Michael. I had really done it this time and was surely in for another whipping. My sister Shay, with a smirk on her face, looked at me and said "That's why you're going to get a whoopin' and I am going to laugh at you! You are so stupid Kim, all you do is get in trouble all day long. That's why you can never go outside!" I looked at my sister with tears in my eyes and screamed, "LEAVE ME ALONE WITH YOUR STUPID ASS! YOU MAKE ME SICK AND I DON'T LIKE YOU CAUSE' YOU ALWAYS TELLING ON ME WITH YO STUPID ASS! AND I DON'T CARE IF YOU TELL, CAUSE' I'M RUNNING AWAY ANYWAY! AND NOBODY'S GOING TO EVER FIND ME EVER!" I licked my tongue out at my sister and ran to get my belongings. "I'm not going to stand around this stupid place and get no whipping, you must think I'm crazy. That's why I should have blew the world up in *the first damn place!"* I cried loudly as I continued placing my clothes in a pillow case. *"That's why I am telling Annie and MA'MA on you cause' you keep cussing and you don't even care!"* stated my sister Shay with excitement. *"I said I don't care who you tell, STUPID!"* I cried, my sister Shay then ran up the stairs and shouted, *"Call me stupid one more time and I'm going to punch you in the face! You're not going to be satisfied until I do!"* I looked at her while still crying and said, *"Do it then, I don't care! I keep telling you to do it!"* All of the adults headed down to Mrs. LeShea's house, to retrieve Michael. When they got there, Mrs LeShea had already come out and the dog was on top of Michael licking his face. Michael was safe and alive, so there was really no need for me to get whooped. After the situation got under control, the adults came back to the house. I didn't get a chance to run away, so I hid behind the couch. However, *MA'MA* still found me because of my big mouth sister. *"Go and get me that switch off the bush and you better get the right one too or I'm going to beat your ass for bringing me one that was too short!"* Shouted *MA'MA*.

Needless to say, I received *yet* another whooping from my grandmother.

A TRIP TO MISS MAY'S SALON

After all of the commotion settled down from the Michael incident and my whipping being over, I just took a seat on the couch. As I was sitting there, my mom came through the door. While she was walking through, I'd noticed how she pushed past her older sister without even saying a thing. For as long as I could remember, my mother and her eldest sister never uttered a word to each other or at least not in my presence. This was very strange to me as a child and I don't think that my grandmother ever made them talk but only they knew why their relationship was so estranged. One could only assume why it was that way but eventually in later years , when the days were few, they would speak again. *Why hold on to a festering grudge, only to regret that you allowed it to grow.* My mother would drop her sister off at work, fix food for the family and everything *yet* she never uttered the smallest word. I guess that would be considered an unfortunate level of sibling rivalry but that's for another story. I sat there on the couch, thinking about how the events of that day unfolded and how Michael was almost mauled to death by Mrs. LeShea's dog. I was so focused on running away and not getting whooped, that I forgot that there was still a strong possibility of me having to go to school. I then jumped up off the couch, stood in front of my mother with my arms folded, with a tear stained face and asked her a question. I had to divert away from the whole school thing, so I asked her *"Mama, why don't you ever talk to Grace?"* That's when my mother looked at me remorsefully, brushing off what I'd just asked and stated, *"Hey, are you girls ready to go and get your hair done? You know you have to go to school Monday? Come on, let's go!"* She said, gathering us girls together to go around to May's to get our hair done. *"Let's*

89

go!" Ms. Mary, who everybody called May for short, was the local hair dresser that everyone in our neighborhood went to for the latest hair styles. I remember walking into the salon, down a flight of stairs and noticing a black and white television set that seemed to only play old western movies. I remember not being able to concentrate on getting my hair done because I was very hungry, I guess all the commotion from earlier gave me an appetite. Ms. May had some snacks, an old pop machine that stayed filled with *Coca-Colas* and a host of other things that could've satisfied my appetite but we could never buy any of it, *cause'* we never had any money. We would watch the other customers eating their chips, their candy bars and drinking their nice cold coke's enviously, wishing we had the change to get some. *"I'm hungry!"* I yelled with urgency *yet* no one seemed to care. My sister quickly looked at me and said, *"Shut up right now before I tell on you when we get home! You always hungry and watch me, I'm going to tell on you when we get home! You make me so sick!"* She shouted before walking over to the chair in front of the black and white television set to watch the western that was playing. My sister then turned, rolled her eyes and stuck her tongue out at me. It was now time for me to get my hair done and I wasn't too thrilled about that. I was a very tender headed child and Ms. May was very rough on my hair. I tried not to cry when she was washing my hair but I couldn't hold it in. *"What's the matter with you Kim? You doing all that crying, aren't you a big girl?"* asked Ms. May, triggering my faint cry's to climb into a scream. Somehow, in the middle of me crying and screaming, I managed to yell *"I'M CRYING BECAUSE YOU KEEP GETTING ALL OF THAT DAMN SOAP IN MY EYES, BURNING THE HELL OUT OF ME!"* Ms. May hit me on my arm and said, *"I'm going to tell Mattie Lee on you for doing all that cussing when I see her! Y'all hear this child over here cussing? You just watch and see! You think that smack on the arm hurt, you just wait until your grandmother gets a hold of your bad ass!"* I looked at her while she began to dry my hair and said, *"You didn't care about my eyes burning any old way, all you care about is talking about people and digging your fingers in that bloody meat that man stole!"* The people in the salon started to look shocked and began to murmur sporadically. My sister looked at me and then said very loudly,

"Ooh, you just wait until we get home! I'm going to tell MA'MA that you were being very disrespectful to Ms. May! You watch and see!" I raised the hair dryer off of my head, looked at my sister and shouted, *"I don't care, tell on me! She never pays attention anyway, she always burning my ears. I should call the cops on her, see how she like that!"* After a brief back and forth with my sister, Ms. May called me back over to her chair, so that she could press my hair. *"I should call the cops on you right now, cause' I know you're going to burn my ear!"* I shouted, hoping she would skip this part of the process. Ms. May looked at me and forcefully asked, *"Who you think you talking to little girl?"* Now any other child probably would've just stayed quiet, especially if they knew their actions would lead them down a road of trouble but... I wasn't that child. *"You, I'm talking to you! (the hot comb hits my ear) Ouch! YOU BURNED ME!"* I cried, flinching while holding my hand up to my hair. *"Stop being so smart and hold your ear down!"* shouted Ms. May, hitting my hand because I continued holding it over my hair. After awhile, our hair was finally done and the

torture I endured was over. My mom had to finish getting our school shopping done, so *MA'MA* came to pick us up from Ms. May's salon instead. I was caught off guard when she arrived and wasn't to thrilled of the possibility of her finding out about the way I acted either. Before I could even devise a solid plan of action to get out of this, wouldn't you know, my sister Shay couldn't wait to be the first one to tell on me. *"MA'MA! Kim was acting so bad, she was talking smart to Ms. Mary and she was cussing! Is Kim going to get a whooping? I think you should whoop her!"* My sister eagerly told on me without any reservation. Ms. May didn't even have a chance to open up her mouth, before my sister Shay started tugging on my grandmother's dress. *MA'MA* kept her composure, calmly walked over to Ms. May and said, *"Hey Ms. Mary, was any of my granddaughters being disrespectful to you?"* My heart began to sink to the bottom of my shoes, I was praying she didn't say anything to my grandmother about me because if she did, I was surely going to tell that she was hitting me and burning my eyes and my ears. Ms. Mary looked at my grandmother and then glanced back at me and said, *"No,*

Kimberly was alright. She just doesn't like getting her hair

done but no Ms. Mattie, she wasn't being disrespectful at all!"

Well, that was a relief, I couldn't believe it. After the way I was

behaving, I just knew she was going to tell on me but she

didn't. I was free and in the clear, so I thought. Of course when

I got home, I got whooped *yet* again. All of my sister Shay's

snitching from earlier, finally paid off.

After my whipping, my grandmother gave me some cereal

because I was still very hungry. I really loved fruit loops, not to

mention there was a doll on the back of the cereal box that I

really wanted. I needed it and I just had to have that doll, so I

got the scissors out of the drawer and cut the image out. I

walked around with that cutout for almost a year. No matter

how much I tried to get my mother to buy me that beautiful

white doll, with golden curly hair and a beautiful flower dress

on, she wouldn't do it. However, she did buy me paper dolls

and that was fine but it didn't take the place of the doll on the

back of the *Froot Loops* box.

When my mom finally made it home from shopping, it was like she was putting on a fashion show. We usually had everything we needed from the help of my dad and one of the charge cards, that my aunt always allowed my mother to use on us three girls. As our little fashion show began, I wanted to try on everything. Of course, my older sisters didn't want anything to do with it but I on the other hand welcomed it. I just knew I was a model, an actress, a singer and I think I even wanted to be a *Soul Train* dancer. My mom would make me try on all of these clothes, mostly dresses because we were not allowed to wear pants. My grandmother would often say, *"Little girls are supposed to look like little girls, not little boys!"* and *"Little boys wear britches and little girls are supposed to wear dresses!"* However, my mom would sneak and buy us pants without *MA'MA* knowing and of course, she would buy me these things that were not quite pants or shorts, they were called *pedal pushers* and they were the hottest thing out.

SCHOOL BEGINS

After a long hot summer, the first day of school had finally arrived. I had dreaded this day all of my life. I'd even devised sinister plans unsuccessfully to prevent this very day from coming, but it still came. *Why didn't those damn teachers go on strike?* I'd thought but oh well, I guess I would have to face this head on. I got up that morning and washed up. My mother wanted me to wear those *pedal pushers* she had gotten me and that's what I was looking forward too. However, since *MA'MA* hadn't left for work *yet*, I ended up having to wear a green and blue plaid dress, with matching green and blue socks. Thanks to my eldest sister Kelly, my hair was in two ponytails. That day, my mom allowed my sisters to leave without me because it would take some convincing, to get me to the place that I despised. She asked my uncle Junior to drop us off at the school and I became more nervous the closer he got. When we arrived, I saw my sisters talking with some of their friends *yet* I didn't have that same luxury. I didn't know anyone *nor* had I been to this school before, with the exception of the free breakfast program last summer. My mother registered me and I was so afraid, so I had to think of something to remove me from this current situation. After the registration process, my mom was given a slip of paper and directions on how to find the classroom that I was supposed to be in. The teacher stood in the classroom doorway, anxiously welcoming the students to the class. As we approached the front of the line, the teacher walked up to me and my mom and introduced herself. I became more frightened because I'd never been in this situation before and to me, that was the scariest part of all. My mother nudged me in the direction of the teacher but I quickly ran behind her, screaming and hollering. I felt as if my mother was trying to give me away to this woman and I wasn't having any parts of that. *"I WANT TO GO HOME! I DON'T KNOW THIS WHITE WOMAN!"* I cried, continuously. My mother got down on one knee so that we could be at eye level and said, *"Don't say that! Don't you want to stay here with the other children and learn?"* she asked, as the teacher looked on in disbelief. I looked at her and screamed, shaking my head vigorously and said *"NOOOO! We've already been here for a long time and I want to go home!"* There was no break in between my cry's and screams, so my mom apologized to the teacher and decided to take me back home. I'd simply cried too much. As we got back to my uncle's car, of course he would have something smart to say about me not staying at school. *"Annie Ruth what is she doing with you? Jimmy (his nickname for me)?"* My uncle Junior asked, surprised at my mother for not making me stay. *"What are you doing getting back in my car? You're supposed to be in school, so what are doing coming back to the car with your mother?"* he asked me *yet* again but I didn't have the answers. *"Since you don't want to go to school and learn, you're sure going to help MA'MA and Debra clean my room, since you want to be a dummy!"* he yelled. My mother looked at him and said, *"Don't call my baby no dummy! She's just afraid and tomorrow is another day. She can start off fresh and she is not cleaning your nasty room!"*

The very next day my mother dropped me off at the front door of the school, *which to me*, marked the beginning of the end. As I stated earlier, I was a very shy child when it came to people that I did not know, so this was a very frightening experience for me. I had a terrible time adjusting to being in school, I wasn't feeling this new experience at all. So after a few weeks, I decide to come up with excuses on *why* I shouldn't go to school. I knew that whatever I came up with had to be clever, if I never ever wanted to go back to that place. Since operation *"blow up the world"* failed miserably, my next plan had to definitely work. The first plan I'd came up with, was standing over the heating vents. The house that I grew up in had heating vents on the floor and the furnace in the home was fueled by coal, this would make the house very hot if the coals were constantly being put into the furnace. This particular furnace was very loud, so I knew when it was coming on because of how abrupt the noise was. I would go over to the vent and stand over the heat until my head got very hot, then I would run to my mother and say, *"Hurry up and feel my head! I'm so hot, I have a fever and I'm sick!"* The crazy thing about that was, by the time she'd feel my head, it had already cooled down. When that didn't work, I would run and hide in the closet but my cousin always seemed to find me. *"Auntie Annie, Lemma is hiding in the closet but she took the diamonds out and you won't be able to save her."* My mother would look at her and say, *"Okay, you know what to do. Go and get me a butter knife, so that I can get her out of the closet."* Once she got me out of the closet, I looked at my cousin and said, *"That's why I don't like you anyway! You never let me play with your barbie dolls and you're always scratching my arms up with those long nails anyway. So, how would you like it if I tell on you? I think you grow those nails like that so you can kill me and I'm going to tell on you, just watch and see!"* My cousin stared back at me and said, *"That's why I have the runaway note you wrote and I'm going to show it to Annie!"* I looked at her and forcefully yelled, *"YOU NEED TO MIND*

YOUR OWN BUSINESS AND LEAVE MINES OUT OF IT!" I

screamed, as I pushed her out of the way and ran to my mother.

I had to think of something fast because I just couldn't go back

to that place. I have been there for over four weeks now.

Nothing seems to be working and this has got to stop. One day

after school, I ran in the house and changed my clothes and

went outside. I gathered all of my friends together and I told

them to get their belongings because we were going to run

away to California to meet Michael Jackson, because he would

help us and we would never have to go back to school. *"Okay,*

everybody listen! If you want to come, you can come but if you

don't, you need to leave right now! I have some diamonds that I

have been hiding from everyone, so I can pay for everybody to

get on the train and we going to California to live with my

cousin." I explained, while they all looked bewildered, *"Who*

is your cousin Kim? Yeah, who is your cousin?" They asked all

at once. I looked at them all and said, *"...Michael Jackson, of*

course! And if y'all would have come to my birthday party

then, y'all would have seen him for yourselves, for your

information!" They all looked at each other with confusion, then one of them confidently hollered out, *"NA'UN! Michael Jackson ain't none of your cousin! You a big liar Kim! Yeah, you're a big liar!"* They all began to shout , I looked at them all and shouted, *"GO HOME THEN!"* Needless to say, they all left murmuring amongst themselves, leaving me behind *yet* again.

After that, I decided to go in the house because I had to re-evaluate my plan. I decided not to run away, so I resulted in hiding one of my shoes. I figured that if I hid one of every shoe that I had, I would never have to go to school. This worked for a while, then my older sisters started to fuss about me making them late for school but that didn't matter to my mom because she made them help her look for my shoe that had mysteriously disappeared. This went on for more than two whole weeks, my plan was finally working, so I thought. My mom, who was growing tired of hearing my sisters complain about not getting to school on time, told them that they didn't have to wait for me any longer and that she would just try to find the shoe on her own. However, my sister Shay was very jealous of the fact that I was able to stay home the majority of the time from school because of my missing shoe and vowed that she'd help find it. Starting the very next day, my sister Shay got up earlier than usual in her efforts of preventing me from missing school. She did this to purposely find my shoe and once she'd found it, she wouldn't let anyone know until the time was right. Shay was determined to bring an end to my successful plan. The science behind this was, I'd wake up and get dressed for school and when my mom said it's time to go, I would say *"I can't find my shoes, there not where I left them! I looked everywhere!"* It wasn't that easy the next time, I was caught red handed! When I went to execute my *"I Can't Find My Shoe"* plan, here comes my sister Shay the detective, with the evidence in hand *"Mama, I found Kim's shoe! It was in the closet!"* My operation was compromised for about two weeks, until one day after school I looked my sister Shay dead in her eyes, I was very close to her face, as close as I could get and whispered *"You always telling my mama on me and that you found my shoes. You need to mind your own damn business and stay out of mines! I'm sick and tired of you and everybody else being in my business!"* Shay looked at me and said maliciously, *"You better get out of my face right now wit yo stank'n tuna breath, before I bust your lip and you ain't got no business and I can do what I want! Who's going to stop me? Certainly not you, miss hide your shoe every day so you won't have to go to school!"* I stared my sister Shay down and said, *"Why are you so worried about me losing my shoes? If my mama wasn't mad, why are you? You're just jealous that you couldn't stay home with my mama and eat ice cream and cake and tuna fish sandwiches and watch tv! WIT' YO UGLY SELF!"*

As the months rolled by, my mother began making a lot of money doing the bookkeeping for the *Numbers Man.* She was now able to buy us more than one pair of shoes, including tennis shoes. *Now, what was a person like me to do?* I guess there would be no more hiding of the shoes for me, I just had to bite the bullet and go to school. I hated that school. Needless to say, I never missed another day of school, *so they thought*. I guess my mother really wanted us to have a good education, the best education, the kind that money couldn't buy.

CHAPTER 4

A ROSE FOR MY MOTHER

"Perfection, the true epitome of a genius. That's who she was!"

My mother was very smart, beautiful and intelligent. A woman who was regal in everything that she did. My mother represented such a high level of greatness, that many people envied her stride. I guess you're wondering why it seems my reference of her is that of an only child, *clearly I'm not*. It's just that me and all of my sisters had this bad habit of calling her *"My Mother"* as if she belonged to each one of us separately, solely and individually. *Mines... [sigh]and mines alone* is what I'd felt. I loved my mother dearly and I'm aware of how I am talking about her in past tense, this is because she is no longer with us. My mother was a very kind woman, there never came a time that she wouldn't lend a helping hand. This served to be a bad thing at times, as many tried to assume or take her passive kind hearted ways as a sign of weakness; but she was far from that. I have never in my life heard her say anything against anyone or bad mouthed anybody, even if they were that way towards her. This even stands true towards her estranged sister, though there was a void there, she never uttered a negative word about her. She would do any and everything in her power, to see that things were taken care of. Despite the troublesome childhood she'd faced in her past and the hopes of a great education being grimly far from view, my mother graduated from high school when she was just 15 years of age and attended the Lewis College of Business thereafter. The brilliance that permeated throughout her mind caught the attention of many other prestigious colleges and a potential career with the Smithsonian Institute, because of her genius like abilities. Unfortunately, this loving and gentle soul would have to give up her collegiate education as well as that job offer from the Smithsonian Institute to raise her children. The worn fabric of reality would eventually set in once she had to work at a cleaners only a couple of blocks from where we lived. After that didn't work out she started working for the neighborhood numbers house doing administrative bookkeeping to make ends meet. In those day's, local number houses served as a way for people in the community to make a few dollars; this went against everything that the *"structured society"* stood for but she had a drive that pushed her to make things work. My mother seen this as a way to utilize her mathematical genius, make ends meet and the *"Numbers Man"* provided her an outlet to do so, she even had her own office. I understand at this point in my life, that working there was probably not the best job for her too hold because of her desires and admiration of becoming a scientist, but I also acknowledge the sacrifice that she made for us. Though working for the *"Numbers Man"* paid her well, it was considered illegal and in many cases frowned upon. This was looked at as a set back, especially compared to the caliber of job offers she'd been presented with in those days. Working there was necessary for her to be able to provide for her family, stay close and not to mention she had become familiar with the atmosphere that many would have deemed as unorthodox. One time, my mother told me that long before we were born, she used to be a cigarette girl at a local club called *The Gray Stone*. She said that she was way too young to work there but she would sneak in all the time to make a couple of dollars. My mother also said that she would wear a short skirt with a pill box hat on and that she'd walk up to patrons in the club saying, *"Cigars, Cigarettes?"* She possessed a lot of ambition, so when it came down to working for the *"Numbers Man"* she knew it would help *MA'MA* pay some bills and provide some funds to raise her children. I know that this is a far jump from working at the Smithsonian Institute and I'm sure the questionable *"Why?"* will sprint through the minds of many of you. Just keep in mind the reality for many great black women in this country who were forced to make sacrifices, still matter. Those who take on trial after trial, burden after burden, aiming to lift the problems of the world from their backs, relinquishing the stressors of the past, present and future, with a child suckling at their bosom as the epitome of God, only to be told that their

aspirations aren't valid, good enough or just doesn't matter...

THEY ALL MATTER!

My mother was my greatest representation of respect and

excellence, I thank her for that. Even though she'd faced her

bouts of hell, I think she'd found comfort in knowing that her

family was heaven to her, especially when it came to us girls.

We served as her peace and sometimes her headache but she

loved us immensely. I remember my mother would sing and

make up stories for us girls. Not only was she a mathematical

genius, she was also a magnificent singer and story teller as

well. I remember how she would tell a story in song form,

through this call and response type of game she'd come up

with called *"Do You Remember?"* She would sing the phrase

♪♪ *Do You Remember?* ♪♪ very beautifully followed by a line

from another song, then we'd have to say and sing the title of

that particular song once we'd recognized it. My mother's

creativity seemed endless to me, I must've inherited my gift of writing and story telling from her. I remember how she had an innate ability to be able to provide mountains of information to us, but once she taught you something, you'd better be able to retain the gems that she'd just bestowed upon you. I would have so many questions for her because I was very inquisitive and the youngest at the time, *however*, sometimes when I'd ask her too many questions or if I'd asked her the meaning of something, she'd always say *"Go look it up in the dictionary!"* As she'd tell us to look things up in the dictionary, my mother would humorously always have one ready. *Yeah, my mother was one of those girls who carried a dictionary with her everywhere, you could always find one in her purse.* She was an amazing and very smart woman!

To my mother, one of the greatest variations of God that blessed this realm with a magnificent zeal of light, I send a divine rose spiritually to you because of the many sacrifices that you made, your undying gratitude, your humaneness on the multiple perspectives of life and your benevolent wisdom. I'm forever grateful for you.

CHAPTER 5

OLD MAID

"A weekend with the Jones's"

As the first semester of school had began to settle and the days seemed to fly bye, I still couldn't quite make any friends. The adjustment from home to school still served as a challenging routine to get used to. I'd mentioned earlier, that I was a very shy girl growing up when it came to folks I didn't know, in school it was worse. Outside of the people in my family or the neighbors on our block who were like family, I didn't really have any connection with anyone. It's not like I didn't want any friends, I honestly just didn't know how to make them or the importance of them while in school. When it came to me really having or making friends, I piggy backed off of my sisters and their associates. Before being in school, I never had to want for any friends or friendship because I had a large family and we all lived in the same home or on the same street. I was fortunate enough to have a host of aunts, uncles and cousins who were my age or just a little bit older. This made me feel as if I didn't need to know how to meet or make new friends, they were always there. I thought that, since I had enough cousins and kids in my neighborhood who were like cousins, It wouldn't be a requirement to have social skills because they were just extra playmates. Somehow, school served as a different thing altogether in that category, it was like night and day with me. I had the biggest mouth at home, with confidence to match it, but at school it was as if my mouth had become mute. For many years, I blamed this on my mother and the type of upbringing we'd had. I felt that because of the way that life was for my mother, her siblings and *MA'MA* while they were in

Georgia, served as the root of why they were so protective of us. I understand the abusive life that they'd faced at the hands of my grandfather, but the level of overprotection that was given hindered us in many ways socially. *Now don't get me wrong*, I loved being around my family because it was so many of us and we were very tight knit but sometimes it was just too much. We weren't allowed to have a lot of outside friends *nor* were we allowed to go to their homes and please don't mention spending the night, that never was going to happen. My mother and grandmother kept a forcefield around our circle, it was hard as *hell* to get in and we were not getting out of it. This has always been a sad situation to me because I never had any friends in school, not until I reached middle school. Before that, no one ever talked to me in school. I would sit by myself, play by myself and even eat lunch by myself. No one ever came over to ask me if I wanted to play and I wouldn't dare ask them if I could play, that was out of the question. I was way too shy to do that. That was my demeanor for awhile, until one day... I spotted him and I had to have him!

As I slept peacefully under my mother (*yes, I was a very scary child and always wanted to sleep in the bed with my mother*), I could hear her sweet voice saying, *"Kimberly wake up, you have to get ready for school."* I sat up in the middle of the bed and wiped the sleep from my eyes, stretched and jumped out of the bed. I ran to the bathroom to get dressed for school, *yes you heard right!* Me, of all people, was ready and willing to go to school without anyone threatening to whoop me if I didn't get my clothes on, or my sister's threatening to leave me because I was taking too long to get ready. Although, I'd usually hope and pray that my mother would allow me to stay home but not today. *Why not today, you ask?* It was because of *him...* Timothy.

The month was October and the only person that was on my mind was Timothy! There was something so intriguing *yet* mysterious about Timothy, he captivated me instantly. I'd never seen anyone like him in my life during that time. Timothy was so fat and round, so jolly and had rosy cheeks just like Santa Claus. I had to have him! I had to see what would happen if I did what I'd been contemplating doing from the very first day that I laid eyes on him.

Over the following weeks, I had devised a plan that I'd thought out precisely and clear. I just couldn't wait to execute it and today, I would get the chance to see him again. With tuna sandwich in hand and with all of the kids including my big mouthed sister Shay talking about me and running away from me because of my tuna sandwich, I stayed focused and nothing else mattered to me. The only thing that mattered was Timothy, he was the person that was on my mind. I couldn't think about anybody or anything else except for Timothy. *Now, I know that you are probably wondering why a 5 year old, yes a 5-year-old, my birthday was right after school started, couldn't think of anything but seeing Timothy, a little boy!* Nothing else intrigued me more during that time.

No holiday or special occasion satisfied my interest or kept my attention long enough to shift my focus off of him. No Halloween would be able to provide me the satisfaction I was after, even though my mother always gave us girls the best Halloween parties. From the many elaborate costumes she'd gotten for us, haunted houses she'd put together, to the mounds of candy we got and the apples we'd bobbed for, just didn't matter to me. Not Thanksgiving either, even though this meant all of our family and friends would be over for a feast after the parade. I didn't have the desire for Christmas or the desire to go meet Santa Claus at the Hudson department store, with their many caroling elves, magazine-like decorations and winter wonderland gift-shop that we would go into, to buy gifts for whomever we'd picked during the family's Christmas gift drawing. My mom was always stuck with buying the most gifts because she had the most children. None of that would wrap me up with excitement, even the joys of finding out where all of our gifts that were supposedly made by Santa's elves and personally delivered to us by a reindeer chauffeured sled, were hidden. We knew that my mom was the one buying those gifts. She always seemed to have all of the gifts hidden all over the house but mostly, behind the couch *yet* to me none of that mattered. I could think of nothing else except for the rosy cheeks of Timothy.

My mother began wondering *why* I seemed to be so preoccupied and felt that I needed someone to play with. I was becoming too restless in her eyes, so she decided to call my aunt Shaky to come and get me *however*, I later found out that my preoccupied mind had nothing to do with why she was sending me away. My mother was sending me off because, *as she put it earlier in this book, "The Rabbit Died!"* and this would be the perfect opportunity for her to break the news to my grandmother. When my aunt finally arrived, my mom had a bag packed for me to spend the whole weekend with my cousin, *even though I did not want to go.* My cousin Achy and I were the same age, I just happened to be older by a few months. She was born in December, which meant she was in a lower grade than I was. This led me to believe that I was better and smarter. I was very mean and rude to her but none of that seemed to matter, she still always wanted to play with me even if I didn't want to play with her. I can honestly say that my cousin really loved me but I couldn't quite stand her. My attitude and behavior towards her stemmed from my grandmother's color struck treatment. As I stated earlier, my grandmother treated all of her lighter skinned grandchildren better and my cousin Achy was lighter, *much lighter than I was*. Psychologically, this made me feel inferior and I unfortunately took that frustration out on her. I was always out to teach her a lesson, a lesson that she never deserved.

As I left to go with my aunt, I still felt very hesitant and uneasy about spending the night over there and it was because of those very reasons I'd mentioned before. Not to mention, I didn't feel like being dead that weekend from food poisoning but I didn't have much of a choice. From the time that I arrived, I felt as if my aunt was trying to poison me. That Saturday morning, my aunt came into the bedroom where her daughter Achy and I were playing and said, *"Lemma, what would you like for breakfast?"* Before I could even get a word out, my cousin Achy shouted *"I want hash-browns, toast and... eggs!"* I looked at her and said, *"She didn't ask you Achy, she asked me!*

I don't like hash-browns!" Achy looked at her mother and shouted again, *"Yes Lemma do Mama, cause' we want the same thing!"* She began laughing hysterically and I instantly started crying. *"Nu'Un!"* I shouted, while jumping up and down. *"I don't like hash-brown, I only want pancakes and nothing else! You shut up Achy! You talking too much and I'm not going to play with you no more cause' you keep saying it!"* I continued to cry inconsolably, before being calmed down by my aunt. *"Don't cry Lemma, Achy stop teasing her before she goes home and never comes back over to play with you anymore! I'll fix you pancakes Lemma, I will fix Achy hash-browns, eggs and toast, is that a deal?...Good!"* Stated aunt Shaky, as she exited the bedroom.

As we sat in the room playing, I realized that this breakfast was taking a little longer than usual to get done. I was very hungry, so I told Achy I was going to the bathroom but ended up in the kitchen talking to my aunt Shaky. While in mid conversation with my aunt regarding school and having friends, I seen her with my very own eyes pouring pancake batter into the same skillet that she used to cook Achy's hash-browns and eggs in. I couldn't believe what my eyes were seeing, This could not be real! *"She is trying to kill me!"* I thought to myself. That's when I knew immediately, that I had to get out of there! Not to mention, she tried to kill me the night before by cooking chicken, mashed potatoes and gravy with peas... *I don't even like peas.* The very thought of me ingesting any type of pea, turned my stomach and would eventually take me out. Besides, my mom never made me eat peas. *Why should I eat the peas that she prepared for dinner? I most certainly was not!* After I sternly opposed eating any peas, my aunt decided to hold me hostage at her dinner table. *"You're not getting up out of that chair until you eat those peas!"* She boldly stated. *Who would do that to a child?* This was very disgusting to me and I wouldn't comply with her demands. I sat at that table for hours, even fell asleep a few times but I still couldn't get up. After my dozing off had turned into a full slumber, Aunty Shaky grabbed me by the arm and told me to go and get ready for bed. I began to whimper and cry but when she walked away to go sit on her husband's lap in the bathroom (*while he sat on the toilet*), I snuck and called my grandmother. When she answered the phone, I began whispering. *"MA'MA it's me, Kim! My auntie is trying to kill me and she in the bathroom sitting on his lap while he using it?"* My grandmother confusingly replied saying, *"I can hardly hear you... Who is this?...Is this you Kim? Who's trying to kill you baby?"* Now that my grandmother recognized it was me who was calling her, I continued whispering. *"MA'MA, it is me! I'm whispering so listen carefully, it's Kim! I can't talk loud or else I'm dead meat! I said Shaky, She's trying to kill me! Please send help for me and fast! I got to go cause' here she come to kill me!"* I swiftly hung up the phone before I was caught by my aunt. After a few moments later, my grandmother urgently called back. *"Hey, bring Kim home! She wants to come home."* Stated *MA'MA.* Shaky, shocked by what she was hearing, replied with concern, *"Why does she want to come home Mama?"* asked Aunt Shaky. *"Hell, I don't know! Something about killings and toilets, listen just bring that child home! I'm sick and tired of her calling me!"* yelled *MA'MA.* My aunt gestured for me to come over where she was sitting and I stood there in front of her while she continued to wrap up the conversation with MA'MA. *"Okay, I'll bring her but definitely not tonight! I will bring her tomorrow. I ain't bringing her tonight mama, cause' I'm tired and I wasn't planning on getting out of my bed tonight."* She said with seriousness, *"Okay, but when you get a chance bring her home or I'm going to send Annie Ruth to get her, cause' the child wants to come home. I don't know why y'all took her in the first place, y'all know how she is!"* MA'MA irritably stated before getting off of the phone. *"Okay, mama!"* After their conversation ended, My aunt Shaky confusingly walked me into her bedroom and asked, *"Why did you call my mama and tell her you wanted to come home? Why did you do that? I know one thing, I'm not taking you tonight! I'll take you tomorrow. Now, you can go and get ready for bed cause' you're not going tonight if I have to take you and I mean that Shit! Get out of my room!"* I quickly exited the room as my aunt continued talking to her husband about what I just did. *"Telling mama that bull fart, that I was trying to kill her, ain't that a blip!"* My aunt and uncle were very disappointed that I wanted to leave and go home and not to stay and play with

123

Achy, they were getting on my nerves. Now, don't get me wrong I really loved them but sometimes my cousin could be so annoying. They were always trying to get me over there to play with her, even when I had plans of my own and I hated when they or when anybody interfered with my plans. I got along with the majority of my cousins but you have to understand what I stated earlier, Achy was lighter than me and I felt she had more things and was treated better. She had the complexion for the protection, *as some would say back then.* On many occasions she, along with my other cousin *Toy*, didn't want me to play with any of their things or barbie dolls and I wasn't having that. Afterwards, there would always be a big fight that resulted in my arms getting scratched up really bad. *I wasn't having any of this bull shit, I wanted to go home!* After leaving out of my aunts and uncles room, I went into Achy's room and began crying. *"What's the matter Lemma? If you want, we can play with my dolls and play old maids and bingo if you want. Please don't cry. Come on, let's go give my dolls a bath!"* said Achy, sympathetically. I looked at her, wiped my eyes and nose with my hands and said in a solemnly low voice,

"Okay, I really don't want to play with you but I will. Only if you let me have your old maid cards and if you don't, I'm not going to play with you all the way, just a little bit!" Achy stared at me without the reservation of sympathy that she'd once shown and said, "No! Tell yo mama to buy you some cause' if I give them to you, I won't have any to play with!" I looked at her and said in a low voice, "You a smart ass and I'm not staying and you or yo mama or daddy can't make me. Now come on and let's play with these dolls!" We then tiptoed into the bathroom, closed and locked the door and began to fill the tub with water. When the tub was half way filled, we threw the dolls in the water and began to splash all over the place. We were screaming loudly and giggling while playing in the tub, when suddenly we heard a deep mysterious voice say, "If I come in that bathroom and y'all playing in that water or got water on anything in there, the both of you are going to get your ass whooped!" It was my Uncle Red's voice, we immediately began panicking. Now, someone much older than or maturer would've said, "Let's drain the water out of the tub and dry everything off, so that we won't get into any trouble!"

Unfortunately (*sigh*), we're talking about five year olds, who thought as children and wouldn't be able to use a high level of common sense. Achy began panicking and said, *"He's going to kill us... Lemma my daddy is going to kill us, cut our heads off and kill us! We've got to get rid of all this water! What should we do?"* I looked at her soaking wet body with fear in my eyes and said, *"Really, Achy? This is all of your fault and MA'MA is coming to get me, so your daddy ain't gone kill me! He gone kill you and kill your mama for having you, cause' you always make a big mess!"* Achy looked at me and said, *"You ain't going home today cause my mama said she ain't taking you, so we both is going to get killed if you don't help me!"* I looked at her and said, *"Nu'Un! My mama or MA'MA is coming to get me so I have to stay alive until... at least tomorrow. Cause' I have to go to school and see Timothy!"* I didn't want to get killed, that would've definitely ruined my chances of seeing Timothy, then it hit me. *"I got a bright idea!"* I shouted, *"You might not like this Achy but it's the only thing that's going to save our lives! Do you want to hear the idea or not? You better say yes or I'm not telling you nothing!"*

I whispered closely to her face. *"Okay Lemma, tell me the bright idea and you better hurry before he comes in here with a big knife!"* I looked at her and whispered, *"Okay, we have to drink all of it! Yep, we have to drink all of the water!"* I whispered and that's exactly what we did, we literally drank all of the water that was in that tub. Looking back, we were probably on the verge of drowning but for and by the grace of God our young lives were spared. Aunt Shaky eventually called out to us saying, *"You girls go and get ready for bed and turn the light out!"* Even though I was scared of the dark, I didn't care if the lights were on or off because I didn't feel good from all of that water we drank. At this point, going home didn't matter. I could survive another night and wait until the morning but I knew one thing, that was I was not ever going to eat any of her food.

The next morning came and I made it through another night. I got up, got in the tub, brushed my teeth and put on my clothes. I walked into my Aunt and Uncle's room and stared at them until I saw some type of movement and said, *"I'm ready!"* My

Aunt who was still in the bed said, *"What are you talking about Lemma, you have to wait until everyone is ready before you leave. Are you hungry?"* She asked. *"I guess but make it cereal because that's safer!"* I replied. My aunt looked at me with a puzzled look on her face, triggering my uncle to burst into laughter while saying, *"She don't like your cooking Shaky!"* Well, I didn't like her cooking but I couldn't let her know that. *"No, it's not that. I just want cereal, that's all."* I stated but the truth and reason why I had to go, was I needed to see Timothy and I didn't have time to be poisoned. I ran into Achy's room and said, *"Let's play Old Maid!"* She looked at me, placed her hands on her hips and sternly said, *"No, cause' you want to go home anyway, so I don't want to play with you and I told you in the first place, tell yo mama to buy you some!"* I Looked at her and said, *"For your information Achy, my mama will buy me some! I probably got some better than your funky cards waiting for me at home! That's why I'm never coming to play with you again and I don't like you and you're not my friend! That's why your daddy gone kill you!"* I rolled my eyes and neck, then I sat down on the floor by the old maid cards. Achy looked at me and yelled, *"I'm telling my mama on you!"* As she ran out of the room, I screamed *"Tell, tell go to jail!"* Once Achy left from around me, I put my coat on and placed the Old Maid cards in my pocket.

It was Sunday and I was ready to get the hell out of there! I had enough of those people, so I sat on the porch with the palms of my hands on my chin and my elbows resting on my knees. I was growing impatient, waiting for my mother to come and pick me up because it seemed to me, that they were not going to ever take me home. After what seemed like a whole eternity of waiting, my mom finally pulled up in a cab. For all she knew, I could have been dead from that hash-brown and peas fiasco but the good thing about everything is that I made it through, I survived. I lived another week to see Timothy and as a bonus, I have the Old Maid cards too. I must say, this weekend turned out better than I could have ever imagined. She owed me anyway! *I mean think about it, I was almost poisoned, I had to eat peas and I drank an entire bathtub full of water.* I wanted those cards so bad, she should have just given them to me. I asked her one more time before I fully went through with taking them, *"Achy, I'm going to give you a chance to be my friend again, can I borrow your Old Maid cards or not? If you say yes, we are friends again and I will come and play with you again for the rest of my entire life but if you say no, I'm never going to play with you! So actually, you should just let me have them and we can be friends forever!"* She looked at me as I chewed my gum and yelled, *"I said no! Tell your mama to buy you some!"* I gave her a chance, so since she want to be like that about it, I'm keeping them! She really pissed me off. I needed to teach her a lesson and on top of everything, I didn't want to play with her anyway! *"Old, ugly African bootie scratcher!"* I shouted. *"I'm telling on you Lemma."* cried Achy and If I can help it, she will never see these Old Maid cards again.

I was finally leaving and I kept the *Old Maid* cards in my pocket but forgot that in one of the pockets, I'd managed to put a hole. Needless to say, as my mom and I were walking out of the house, Aunt Shaky and cousin Achy followed suit. This was something that I was not expecting. *"Mama, why they coming with us? I got to go to school tomorrow!"* My mother looked at me and said, *"Kimberly, stop acting like that! They can come with us if they want!"* I looked at my mother and said, *"Fine, but I'm not playing with her because I just seen them for a million days and I'm tired of seeing her!"* We all climbed in the cab and I told Achy not to sit next to me, however, she did anyway. We finally arrived home and I was not expecting for them to come along or stay with us, I was so angry. *How was I supposed to play with the Old Maid cards with her there and in my face the entire time?* I wasn't even thinking about my sister Shay asking me where I got the cards from, because if she did, I was going to tell her none of her beeswax. I knew that my aunt and cousin were going to stay awhile and probably not leave until it was time to go to sleep, so I wasn't going to be able to play with the cards until tomorrow anyway. This meant I had all night and all day to think about where I could say I got the cards from. *"God, they make me sick!"* I jumped out of the cab before anyone else could and I started running as fast as I could. I didn't even care if a car was coming or not, I just knew that I needed to hide those *damn* cards. I heard my aunt Shaky shouting for me to stop hysterically, *"Lemma wait! Wait Lemma!"* However, I continued to run across that street as fast as I could. Once I'd made it to the middle of the street, the *Old Maid* cards slipped through the hole in my pocket and hit the ground with precision. You could just imagine the look on my face as the cards scattered in the middle of the streets. I was so embarrassed, *What was I to say?* I was cold busted of course. I was such a great little story teller at the time and could easily come up with an excuse at the drop of a dime. They all stopped and looked at the cards in the middle of the street. All I could hear was my cousin Achy saying, *"Ooh, you're in big trouble Lemma, cause' you stole my cards!"* As we all walked in the house, my mother looked at me and commandingly said *"Explain yourself Kimberly!"* I looked at her with tears in my eyes and exclaimed, *"Mama, but... but I didn't take them! You always blaming me for everything!"* I cried loudly, while jumping up and down. *"Then how did they get in your pocket, Kimberly?"* I thought long and hard about how I should answer my mother, I had to turn the tables. *"I don't know how they got in my pocket, maybe Achy put them there!"* Achy looked at everyone involved and began to cry. *"Nu-un, I told Lemma she couldn't play with them no more and she couldn't have them. I told her to ask you to buy her some!"* she cried. I looked at them and instantly screamed and cried too, *"She's a big fat liar, just look at her face! She put them there and she knows it! She's just trying to get me in trouble! Ooh, she make me so sick!"* That was my story and I was sticking to it and after all of that, she still wanted to play with me. Achy still wanted me to come over and play with her on the weekend but none of that was happening unless she agreed to let me have her *Mrs. Beasley* doll!

"Lemma, come and play with me!" I looked at her and said, *"No Achy! I have school tomorrow and plus you lied on me and said I stole your cards and I didn't. You know you put them in my pocket, just trying to get me in trouble and all I wanted to do was look at the pictures on the cards and play with them for a minute and you didn't let me so... I'm going to bed, so I can*

get up for school cause' I have to see Timothy for your

information!"

None of these things would have ever happened, had it not

been for my mother sending me away because of that stupid

rabbit dying and her having to break this news to my

grandmother.

The next morning had arrived and I was eager to get back to

school but something seemed a bit off. I was dressed for

school and had been patiently waiting for my mother to come

down the stairs and give me my tuna sandwich before my

sisters left me. Suddenly, I heard her voice calling for me to

come here, *"Kimberly, come here! I need to show you*

something!" Could she have a gift for me? I thought, so I

immediately ran to the stairs and said, *"Where is it? Where is*

my present?" That's when my mother lifted up her shirt and

excitingly said, *"Look Kimberly!"* I was bewildered, *where*

were my gifts? I looked at her with confusion and said, *"Why*

are you so fat? What's in your stomach?" At this very moment, my mother decided to reveal to me that she was pregnant, *"You're going to have a little brother or sister!"* She shouted with excitement. I screamed uncontrollably, *"NO!!! I DON'T LIKE YOU OR THAT BABY!"* I shouted, before running to my grandmother. For the longest time, my mother told me that I was the baby and if this were the case, *what was she doing pregnant again? "MA'MA, she is having another baby and I don't want no stupid baby!"* I cried *"Who told her she could do that? Did you tell her MA'MA? I ain't never going to school no more and I'm leaving this stupid place!"* I couldn't wrap my finger around how this could've happened but it was becoming very clear that this is what she meant by saying, *"The Rabbit Died!"* I couldn't come to grips with this at all and my grandmother was getting tired of it. That's when she looked at me and said, *"You are acting so ugly, get yourself together, put your shoes and coat on and then go and apologize to your mother! Did you hear me Kimberly? Go and apologize to your mother!"* I looked at my grandmother and said, *"Okay but I don't like this one bit and I don't think that I'm going to have a good day at school. MA'MA, I don't even want my tuna* sandwich no more!" My grandmother looked at me and sternly said, "Make haste and do what I told you to do! Annie Ruth, come and get this child! I don't know why you picked this time to tell her. Y'all go on and go to school, your mother is going to take Kimberly. Go on now before you late!" MA'MA instructed my sisters to go on with out me. Before they left, my sister Shay looked at me and said, "You're so stupid, that's why you make me sick! You know you're just trying to stay home, cause' you don't want to go to school dummy and how do you think I felt when she brought you home? That's why you're not going to be the baby anymore!" Shay laughed at me and ran out the door. My mother finally came down the stairs and said, "Kimberly, I'm sorry. Look at me! You know that you're still my baby, right? I love you. Come on let's go!" As my mother and I walked out of the front door, I turned, waived goodbye to my Grandmother and we left. With my tuna sandwich in my right hand and my mother holding my books and trying to hold my left hand, she walked me to school. Even though I was still very upset and didn't want her to continue to try to hold my hand, she held on tightly. We continued walking to my school and as soon as we got to the building, I quickly snatched away from my mother and took off running. I was just that angry with her and it didn't matter if she still had to come inside of the school because I was late, *none of it was my fault.* After my mom received a tardy slip from the school office and walked me to class, I sat down in my seat and she left... *What a morning!*

CHAPTER 6

TIMOTHY

"Not all that's jolly, is sweet."

From the moment I arrived to school on this special day, my focus was off. I did not pay attention in my class at all, I just couldn't concentrate. It was as if my body had been placed on autopilot, while my thoughts did sprints throughout my head. Despite the news that my mother hit me with earlier, it was still Timothy who absorbed every last one of those thoughts that tried coming into mind. I knew that this day would take the place of all other school days that had come before it, the stakes were just that high. This was going to happen one way or another.

By lunchtime, my mind was made up on what had to be done and the plan I needed to execute in order to succeed. Once we all ate lunch, the bell abruptly began to ring and the Teacher stood up and said, *"Okay class, it is time for recess. Please line up."* It was showtime and there would be no room for error, I had to get this right. To me, there was just no turning back now, I'd invested too much time on this matter. I eagerly rushed to line up for recess and didn't lag my stride. Normally, I never wanted to go on the playground for recess because I didn't have any friends *nor* did anyone ever want to play with me, this day was surely different. When those doors opened to release us onto the playground, I immediately ran to the monkey bars as fast I could. I'd reserved those monkey bars as apart of my plan and didn't need anyone getting in the way of a spot I'd been scoping out for months. I needed to have a clear view of Timothy and those monkey bars gave me the vantage point to do just that. From that position, I could see the entire playground and everyone on it, so no other spot would suffice. With my socks rolled down, I climbed those monkey bars, locked my legs to hold on and began swinging upside down rapidly, while stalking Timothy's every move. I was like a lioness out hunting along the Serengeti, awaiting the perfect opportunity to pounce. I stealthily observed his every move, no matter where he was positioned or what he was doing on that playground. My eyes followed Timothy keenly as he ran around playing with the other children, trying to catch them without enough energy or speed, he was just too fat. In my mind, he was like a baby elephant who'd fallen behind it's herd and readily available to be prey. I wanted him, I needed to have him and today would be that day. As I continued hanging upside down, the world began to slowly turn and I gradually started feeling sick. The bell was taking longer than usual to ring and it seemed I'd been hanging upside down like a bat in a cave, since the time my teacher first dismissed us for recess. I patiently waited for the bell to ring while still in this position, with my ponytails swinging, my coat as well as my dress hanging over my chest, with all of the blood rushing to my head. I was determined to see this through. *[school bell rings]*... When the bell finally rung, I jumped down from the monkey bars and instantly felt really dizzy. With the world around me spinning like a tornado, I dropped to my knees because my equilibrium was off from hanging on for so long. I had to gather my composure because I knew there was no turning back now. I either had to do it or miss the opportunity of a lifetime. My teacher came to the door and said, *"Children please take your place in line."* Now, usually I would have been the first person in line on any other day because I never played with anyone. I'd just sit by the door and wait for the bell to ring. I knew the process very well and knowing that, I'd already calculated Timothy being last in line. All of the children had gone into the school building with the exception of Timothy and I. As he began running, *in what seemed like slow motion towards me*, I stood on the side of the door pretending I was waiting to let him in. I had a hidden agenda and my intentions were not good. I watched Timothy like a hungry wolf who'd spotted its prey as he continued running towards me sloppily, with his coat hanging off of his arms and with it partially dragging across the ground. With a huge goofy smile on his face, slobber dripping from his lips, Timothy finally made it to the door and tried to pass me. I licked my lips, dodged him out and blocked his entrance. Timothy was thrown off by this and said, *"Move out of my way Kimberly or else I'm telling on you!"* I looked at him and said, *"Make me, you don't tell me what to do! You're not my momma or my daddy and I'm not moving nothing for your information!"* I must've gotten under his skin because he turned red. Timothy looked at me with his fist balled up and shouted, *"I said move Kimberly! You had better get out of my way and get away from me now!"* I closely approached him and said sinisterly, *"You better shut up right now or else you're never going to go in that school or see your fat momma and daddy again, ever Timothy! You're just a big dummy"* I started to sense the fear in Timothy and the look in his eyes began to show it. *"Forget you! Your ugly self and I'm telling on you if you don't let me past!"* Shouted Timothy before fearfully screaming for our teacher, I then immediately grabbed him and placed my hand over his mouth. I could feel him trembling, I had him right where I wanted him. *"Didn't I tell you to shut up? You think I'm playing with you? And Timothy, your whole generation is ugly, including you with your fat self and forget you forgot you, never thought about you. Give me a piece of paper and I'll write all about you and your whole entire family is stupid and fat including you... and if you keep trying to tell on me, I'm going to kill you and your family!"* I shouted. Timothy with fear in his eyes, looked at me and shouted, *"Get out of my face and I'm going to count to ten and you had better move out of my way or else!"* Timothy began to count *"1,2,3,4,5..."* Before he could finish counting, I'd halted his speech. *"SHUT UP! You better shut up right now!"* I shouted but he continued to scream out. With my adrenaline rushing through my head, I went for it. I had him cornered and trapped, I wasn't about to let him slip away, not now. I'd given him a warning that he refused to take. With teeth clinched, I grabbed his face as hard as I possibly could and began pinching his cheeks. He began to scream out for help but I wouldn't let him go. In the midst of Timothy struggling to get away and evade me, I'd pounced on him. I had him by the shirt and the more the struggle intensified, the more ferocious I became . It was like I was in a trance and before you know it I bent down and bit Timothy as hard as I could on his stomach. *{LOUD SCREAM}...*

"AAAAAHHHH!!!" screamed Timothy, releasing one of the loudest and piercing sounds that I'd ever heard. I began to cover his mouth with both of my hands but it was too late, Timothy's cries for help had alerted the ears of the teacher and she came to his rescue. Our teacher urgently came over and investigated the situation with concern. *"What happened? Timothy are you okay? Kimberly, what happened to Timothy?"* She asked. I stood there with my hands on my side looking down at the ground, as Timothy was crying too hard and loud. We entered into the school and I walked nervously over to my seat, not knowing if he would tell on me or if he'd remembered what had just taken place. To me, he was just that dumb. I sat in my seat apprehensively, as I watched the teacher calm Timothy down and ask him what really happened. Timothy didn't hold back, he told everything. He told her I'd pinched his face, bitten him on the stomach and wouldn't let him inside of the school. Fear began to take over my whole being, as the Teacher called me over to her desk. I approached her slowly, I heard my Teacher say, *"Kimberly, go out into the hallway and wait for me!"...(slight pause)..."Why?"* I asked, *"I*

didn't do anything wrong. He's lying on me!" The teacher

stared at me with a malicious look on her face and said, *"Did I*

say you did anything? Do as you are told and go and stand in

the hall by the door. Right now Kimberly!" I stood there,

unable to move and that's when she quickly grabbed me by my

arm, leading me out of the classroom, into the hall while the

other children fearfully looked on.

Now, in this day and age I would have been reprimanded or

arrested for assaulting Timothy but back in those days, the

teachers *as well as the principle* were the authority. They

served as the jury and the judge, your fate and destiny rests

within their hands. They meant what *they* said and said what

they meant and you'd better not tell a lie or back talk, other

wise you're going to get a taste of *Mr. Feel Good.* That was the

name of the paddle or the *"whipping stick"* that bad children

got a taste of for misbehaving in school.

Many parents were in total agreement of this treatment and

would get you again once you got home. Then again, that was a time long ago when this type of corporal punishment was acceptable. My teacher immediately went back into the classroom after escorting me out. I would have to spend the remainder of the day in that hall, awaiting whatever punishment I were to receive. I stood there thinking of excuses I could say in my defense, to why I was removed from the class but to no avail. I just couldn't reveal the real reason for my actions, no one would ever believe it. No one in their right mind would buy that my only reasoning for doing what I did, pondered the way I pondered or planned the way that I planned, was all done in order for me to see if Timothy... taste sweet. Before you judge me, keep in mind that I was a child, *so*, I thought he might've taste sweet because of how gleeful and jolly he was. *Now, would you go for that? No you would not!*

I stood in that dark hallway for what seemed like a couple of hours, suddenly, I spotted my sister Shay running down the hallway in my direction. See, Shay was the person that my mom put it charge of walking me home and if I was not ready, she'd surely leave. *"What's wrong with you Kim? Why are you standing in the hall crying? I know you did something!"* I looked at my sister and said, *"That stupid teacher don't like me cause' I'm black, and that dumb fat little boy named Timothy told her a lie! He said that I bit him on the stomach and pinched his cheeks and wouldn't let him come into the school after recess. I didn't do nothing, he lied on me!"* I cried but my sister Shay wasn't buying any of that. *"I'm telling on you!"* She shouted, *"I knew it! You're always doing something you ain't got no business doing. You watch and see! That little boy ain't lying on you, anyway I heard you talking about him for a long time and if you ain't standing outside when the bell rings, I'm going to leave you and you can walk home all by yourself! Miss I ain't do nothing!"* My sister turned and began running in the opposite direction, down the hall. Her leaving me, scared me more than the trouble I would be facing. *"You know good and well, I don't know my way home from this stupid school!"* I screamed. My sister Shay turned around and started jogging backwards, *"So what! You shouldn't have done what you done to get into trouble and like I said, if you ain't outside when the bell rings I'm leaving!"* This made me so furious with my sister. I was very bothered by hearing those words come from her mouth, she never took my side for anything. I guess that's what big sisters are for, not walking you home when they know good and well, that you don't know your way home and you can't walk pass the witches house yourself. I guess her main mission in life, is to tell on me and to get me into trouble, just so I can stay away from her. *"If she leaves me, I'm going to get her back! I'm going to show her and she's not going to like the outcome!"* I continued standing nervously in the hall, awaiting my punishment from the teacher. I became very remorseful of what I'd done to Timothy (*not really*), I shouldn't have done that but now I'm sorry. His stomach didn't taste of sweet candies, cakes or *Froot Loops* like I'd imagined it would. It was very bitter and really salty but his cheeks were extremely soft. I'd become restless standing out there but more importantly, I became very worried that my sister was going to leave without me and plus, I had to *pee*. *"She's going to leave me by myself!"* I cried, as I jumped up and down continuously trying to hold my *pee*. I couldn't help but think about how

148

scary it would be if she'd kept that promise and now because Timothy told on me I'm in trouble with that stupid teacher, *with his salty tasting self.*

"Now, what lie can I tell the teacher so I won't get in trouble?" I whispered, *"Would I tell her that he hit me first? Nope that wouldn't work, she knew that I would never let that happen. I know, I'll tell her that he ran and in the middle of him running he fell and that's how he got those marks on his stomach and cheeks and I'll tell her his face is red because he was crying so hard from falling and I tried to help him up. Yeah, that's what I'll tell her!"* I had my mind made up on what explanation I'd give my teacher but *man, oh man,* the thought of my sister Shay leaving me was starting to affect me . *"Please God, don't let her leave me here by myself! I don't know my way home, plus a dog or a witch might get me. Please help me, amen!"* After I said my prayers for millionth time, the teacher walked into the hall and asked, *"Kimberly, do you understand why you had to stand in the hall, away from the other children?"* I looked down at the ground and said, *"No, I don't understand."*

The lies that I had come up with earlier totally slipped my mind, my Teacher was very intimidating and made me so nervous. *"Well, you do realize that you are to keep your hands to yourself at all times and, at no time on this day or in the future are you to bite anyone! That is a terrible thing to do! Not to mention, all of the germs that is involved with you biting or putting your mouth on someone. Do you understand me?"* The Teacher shouted. I looked at her nervously and said, *"Yes!"* She then looked at me and forcefully said. *"You are going to apologize to Timothy and stay away from him!"* I looked at her with tears in my eyes, thinking I had gotten off with a warning and replied, *"Okay!"* ...Unfortunately, I wouldn't be getting only a verbal warning. *"You are not a savage Kimberly. Now, hold your hand out!"* Stated The Teacher sternly. I looked at her and said *"For what?"* Then without warning, The Teacher grabbed my hand, bent it backwards as far as it could go and once my inner knuckle bones were exposed, she gave me three of the hardest hits this side of heaven. I went into complete shock. *"Never again, bite anyone and don't tell your mother I hit you!"* The Teacher then walked away. I couldn't say anything *nor* was I able to gather myself. The only thing that I was able to do at that time was to jump up and down with my mouth wide opened *yet* no sound came out, I'd been painfully silenced. The Teacher suddenly turned around, looked at me and said very aggressively, *"You better not tell your mother and you better not cry! I had better not hear a sound come out of your mouth! How do you think Timothy felt when you bit his stomach and pinched his cheeks?"* All I could do was shake my head from side to side, as to gesture the response *"No"*. I know what I did to Timothy was wrong and I can admit that remorsefully but what I did to him, wasn't nearly as brutal as the pain I was feeling from being hit by The Teacher. I was only a child, I didn't have any massive amount of strength to do any severe damage to Timothy or anyone else for that matter. It was as if, that teacher was used to beating little black children. When she hit me, she used such force. I know she had to have a vendetta against me. My hand could've potentially been damaged by the way she bent it back, this was very excessive. I couldn't move it *nor* could I readily ball up my fist but *do you think that I told my mother, that white lady hit my hands until they broke off of my body and ran out of that*

school? I should say not, but you know who did...my sister

Shay, even though she said she wasn't going to wait on me, she

did. *"I'm telling and you're going to be in big trouble when*

you get home! I'm telling my mama on you and I'm going to

tell MA'MA!"... and that's exactly what she did, she told. Once

we got home, my sister Shay told my mother everything that

happened and my mother told my grandmother. It was one

thing to give me a warning or some type of verbal

reprimanding but the line was crossed when that white woman

had the *audacity* to whoop me like I was one of her ancestor's

slaves, this infuriated my grandmother the most.

The very next day *MA'MA* and my mother got dressed to

accompany me to school. My grandmother wanted to know

why that white woman had hit my hands the way that she did.

They'd noticed how I could barely move my hand but of

course, I didn't want to tell them what really happened. They

knew that it was something more to the story because of the

way I was acting, I just couldn't tell them. I told them that

152

Timothy hit me on the way in from recess. The teacher didn't notice because she went in the school before any of us. I'd also told them that, she was mean to me because Timothy was *almost* white and I was *all the way* black, I was just protecting myself. Of course, this upset the both of them but mostly *MA'MA*. We'd arrived at the school and my mother and *MA'MA* both escorted me to class. The Teacher wasn't expecting to see them because she told me not to speak a word of this to my mother. I could tell that she was very afraid, you could see the fear in her eyes. The moment of truth had now come and it was my word against Timothy's, the conference was brought to a close but not before my grandmother gave that teacher a piece of her mind. With confidence, poise and strength, *MA'MA* stated to the teacher *"You better not ever put your hands on my grandchild again! I don't care what she did! If you put your hands on her, I'm gone' put my hands on you and see if you like. If my grandchild does anything wrong, call me and I'll deal with her!"* As *MA'MA* walked away, I heard her exclaim *"The nerve of that white woman, puttin' her hands on my grand baby, I bet she won't do that again!"* My grandmother lit her cigarette and walked away, she surely let my teacher have it. I didn't have any more problems from her but I surely wasn't off of the hook just yet.

As soon as we got home my grandmother said, *"Go and get me a switch off of that bush!"* Based solely off of what Shay had told her, I got a whooping. I was so tired of *MA'MA* telling me to get a switch off of those bushes, I contemplated calling the city to cut them down myself. The city needed to come and cut those bushes down anyway because they where very dangerous and created a blind spot. This led to frequent accidents on that corner, so not only was those bushes a danger for me but to all of the motorist and pedestrians who crossed at that corner. After that whooping, I'd vowed to never ever do that again but still... *I lied.*

A SUMMER STRIKE

I made it through the first year of school and that was the end of first grade for me. I just couldn't wait to be promoted to the second grade and it would be here in no time. I just knew that I would be ready and prepared, because I'd gotten used to all of the children at the school. Despite still not having friends, I was a veteran now at this school and even though I wanted friends very badly, I was still too shy to make them outside of the ones in my neighborhood. *"Maybe next year or after this summer, I'll be able to make friends."* I thought.

Summer was fast approaching and this meant, our vacation was right around the corner. I was very excited and nothing could stand in the way of that, not even the slightest fear of potentially getting beat up on the last day of school could stop my stride. Now, I'm sure many of you have heard of these types of occurrences happening or rumored to have happened on the last day of school, when *someone* was going to get beat up and not enjoy their summer. Well, that was the rumor going around my school. Allegedly, the culprits had a large list of children they were going to assault or beat up and somehow my name made the list, *"Damn, I made the list?"* For the life of me, I didn't understand why I'd made it however, I wasn't having any of that *nor* was I about to stick around to find out if it were true or not. I decided to stay very close to my sister Shay, to prevent those mysterious kids who were after me, *for reasons unknown*, from getting near me. Their murmurs wouldn't affect the excitement I'd developed for summer vacation. Even though I didn't want to travel down south and dreaded the thought of it, I was still very excited. *Why was I so excited, you ask?* Well, if you've been following along on this journey, you should know the reason remains the same and that reason is *"I HATED SCHOOL!"* So, *Bon Voyage*!

The first few weeks of summer went along as planned but by the time midsummer came around, there were talks of schools going on strike *yet* again. This time, if the teachers went through with striking or their demands weren't met, our summer vacation would be extended. That was fine by me, school wasn't supposed to begin for another month and a half anyway. Maybe they'll follow through this time, unlike the time when I was going to blow up the world if they didn't but we'll see. Though the schools were out and considered striking, this didn't stop the free food program that the *Black Panther Party* had in place for our community. In the summertime, they still had the free breakfast and lunch program in full rotation. As I stated earlier on in this book, this particular program was quintessential for the development of the youth in our area, those who were less fortunate or did not have a fair chance beneath the foot of a dominant *yet* corrupt society. Even though we always had food, we went to get a free meal. *Why not go and get what was offered for free?* I think, it was more about the fellowship of the community and our love for the people that pulled us together. It was a beautiful and wonderful thing, that someone who looked like me, had skin like me, had hair like mines and my facial features, wanted to give my mind, body and soul nourishment. Understand, there was a lot of poverty in our neighborhood and even if we didn't always know it, we had the instinct to naturally survive by any means necessary. I must admit, we were so rich and wealthy within our spirit and community, that I never knew that we were considered poor. Of course, we didn't have large money bags full of golden coins like the monopoly man but we always had what we needed. I had everything I wanted and never went hungry, we had plenty of food but others weren't as fortunate in that way. Many of them would go without the nourishment they needed to survive. One day, I tagged along with my sister Shay and a few of her friends to go get a free lunch. The majority of the time, I thought those bags would have some candy in them but that was just wishful thinking. It would take for me to become a little bit older and mature, to fully understand the importance of the nourishment they were offering. They wanted us to be healthy or at least not hungry. In my bag, I always got a bologna sandwich with no type of

Miracle Whip or any other condiments on it and an orange.

Back then, I didn't really appreciate it or took for granted what was being offered. I thought it was a waste of my time but for those other kids, you would have thought they had cake and ice cream in those bags. Their level of humility was unmatched and awe-inspiring. They were very appreciative and thankful for the contents in those bags and eating that lunch. It brought them such a great level of joy, to be able to eat amongst their friends and afterwards sing inspirational songs or spark inspirational chants of black excellence. It was in their blood and within their culture to come together. Nowadays, I would gladly embrace that sandwich and orange.

As we walked from the lunch room after standing in a long line to receive our free lunch, we began to play around looking in our bags to see what we would keep and what we would throw away... *Don't judge me, I was young damn it!* We turned the corner and saw the teachers and staff walking with their picket signs held high in the air, fighting for whatever was due unto them. All I knew is that, it was a very beautiful hot summer day and with them on that picket line, we would have some extra time to play *Mother May I, Red-Light, Green-Light!* and who could forget *Frozen Tag* or staying out until the street lights came on. We swiftly walked past the teachers, that's when my first grade teacher spotted me and gestured for me to come over. This caught me off guard, I wasn't expecting to see her and besides, she didn't like me like that. *"Kimberly, come here sweetie!"* She ecstatically shouted, while still speaking amongst her colleagues. *"She was one of my favorite students, so talented. Why don't you sing a song for us, how about Diana Ross and the Supremes?"* I looked at her with reservations until my sister Shay and friends persuaded me to sing. I began singing Diana Ross and the Supremes *"Love Is Like an Itching In My Heart"* loudly. *"♫ The love bug done bit me and I didn't mean for him to get me! ♫"* I sung freely and effortlessly, until she creepily grabbed me by the arm and tried to make me stay with her and for reasons I am not sure of. All I can remember is my sister Shay screaming at the top of her lungs, *"RUN KIM, RUN!"* and I did. With my heart pounding in my chest rapidly, we ran so fast away from them. All I could do was scream loudly, *"That teacher was trying to steal me!"* My sister looked at me while we were all breathing hard and out of breath from running so fast and said, *"I'm glad that you got away, cause' I don't know how I could have explained to my mama and MA'MA what happened to you!"*

<u>NO WAY HOME</u>

The teacher strike that could have done away with school forever, had come to a close. I was now in the second grade and for the life of me, the only thing that I can remember is wearing my older cousin's shoes. These particular shoes were called *Clogs* but nowadays they are called *Wedges,* they were 6-inched heels and I wanted to wear them for my pictures. I remember it being autumn and a lot was going on that day, my eldest sister Kelly was scheduled to be performing in the school talent show and I was taking pictures. My mom came up to the school to inform the teachers that we'd be moving soon, so we would be transferring to another school. My mother kept this a secret, we weren't informed about the whole moving thing until the actual day came. After she'd left from informing our teachers about us leaving, my mom saw me running down the hall in those 6inch heels. She'd spotted me with my clothes hanging off of my body and my hair sticking straight up in the air, like I'd been electrocuted by something. The first thing that came out of her mouth was, *"What are you doing with those shoes on?"* I was shocked to see her standing there, she caught me by surprise. *"Shell... let me wear them!"* I hesitantly replied. The fact of the matter was, my older cousin Shell didn't have a clue that I'd taken them or was even eyeing her shoes in the first place. *"Kimberly, where are your shoes? Go and get your shoes and take those off!"* I turned and ran towards my locker, in order to do what my mom had commanded me to do. My mother didn't wait around for me to change shoes or to get out of school, she told my sister Shay to bring me home instead. Now, I thought my sister Shay heard my mother loud and clear, when she said for her to bring me home but it must've slipped her mind or something because... (*sigh*) she left me. The last thing I can remember about that day wasn't my cousin's 6inch heels or the pictures I'd taken but standing outside of the school crying so forcefully loud and abruptly hard, that I *peed* on myself. My sister Shay had left me just like she had promised to do on so many occasions and no one was there to pick me up. It was very cold and the rain had mixed with the snow and I was soaking wet. I didn't know what to do, I never knew my way home from that school, even though it was just two blocks down. I cried and cried for what seemed like an eternity, I just knew that someone would kidnap me. After awhile, my mother finally noticed that I had not come home with my sister from school and began to worry. When my mother seen my sister she said, *"Sherri, where is Kimberly?"* Shay looked at my mom and said, *"I don't know!"* My mother, in a panic, looked at her and shouted, *"Didn't I tell you to bring my baby home from school! Oh, my God! Junior, please take me to get my baby!"* My mother was furious with my sister Shay for leaving me, *"You did that on purpose. I'll deal with you when I get home!... [leaving out of the door]... Left my baby up at that school, bye herself!"* My mother immediately jumped in the car with my uncle Junior and they rushed to pick me up from school. I had never been so happy to see my mother in my life, *yet* I was still very upset and not to mention, I was soaking wet. *"Jimmy, did you pee, pee on yourself? Annie Ruth, you better hold your child cause I don't want all that piss on my car seat!"* stated my uncle Junior, humorously. My mom picked me up and sat me on her lap in the front seat of my uncles' car and we went to *Park's Bar-B-Q*, then we went home. As we were riding, I turned to my mother and said, *"Mama, can I have some of your barbecue?"* My mom looked at me and said, *"I cooked you some chicken and rice, plus you don't like barbecue bologna."*

BARBECUE ON LILLY BRIDGE

T he day had come for us to move from the North End of Detroit and I was finally through with the second grade, *what a relief.* It was the summertime and summer vacation was in full swing. The thought of me going to a new school once it was over, was the furthest from my mind. I just wanted to enjoy the moments a little while longer. My life on the North End of Detroit was all I'd ever known and living on the Westside of Detroit, was going to take some time to get used to. It was as if I'd entered into a new world on the Westside, it was just that different. It was nothing like living on the North End, *which was a predominantly Black neighborhood with the exception of the hookers and the convenience store owners.* Now we were living in a middle class area with mostly White and Jewish people. Despite not really wanting to leave the North End, I can truly say I loved the house we were moving to. It was like we were moving into a mansion, compared to what I was used to. The old house that we lived in on Marston Street was called a terrace. Some would call it a condo today, that had 4 floors and over 2000 square feet. It was a very big and spacious home, *however*, it came with many problems and challenges. It was filled with lots of rats, which I'd never seen with the exception of the baby pigs being under the front stairs and roaches, that I would only see occasionally in the kitchen. No one would've ever known that it had the problems it had, because my grandmother kept it exceptionally clean. Now, the house that we moved into was on a street called Ilene and it looked so clean and it smelled wonderful, *not like our last house*. Even though our new place looked nice and was in a considerably nicer area, it came with a whole set of new rules that would surely take some time to adjust to. One rule in particular, that still stands to this very day is, we were not allowed to barbecue in this new neighborhood. I remember my grandmother saying, *"Ain't no bar-b-q'n going on over here at this house! These white people don't do that, they don't eat barbecue!"* For as long as I lived in that house, there was no cooking outside at all and if my mom wanted to barbecue, we would have to go over to one of my aunts houses for all summer festivities and holidays. Most of the time we would go to Belle Isle and my mom, along with her sister Mattie Pearl, would round up all of the kids and we would play games and they would cook on the grill for hours. Sometimes, they'd cook into the middle of the night but It was always a hassle though. You see, my Aunt and Uncle were both heavy drinkers and it never failed, every time before we would go to Belle Isle, there'd be an altercation between them. They would drink excessively and listen to the blues, *mostly BB King records*. Then they would start crying and before you knew it, my aunt would go upside my uncle's head, then that's when the guns would come out... *literally*. They both would grab guns and everyone would take off running. My mom would gather up all of her children and put us in the car, while my aunt commenced to beating my uncle up. Instead of taking us home, we would leave in that station wagon and go to Belle Isle, as if nothing ever happened.

I remember on one occasion, during one of the hottest days of the summer, my mother wanted to barbecue for us because it was a beautiful day but again, we were not allowed to barbecue at the house we lived in with my grandmother. So, we went to my aunt Mattie's house on the Eastside of Detroit. She lived on a street by the name of Lilly Bridge and we would go over there all the time. My mom and aunt were in the back yard setting up tables and getting the grill ready for cooking. My uncle was working, so it probably wouldn't be as interesting as it could be. I was with some of my cousins in the basement, jumping and doing flips on an old dirty mattress. Call me mischievous but that day, I needed for some serious action to take place. I knew that without my uncle around, there would be minimal drinking, no listening to *"The Thrill Is Gone"* by BB King, no crying or fighting or even pulling guns out on this day. I needed to instigate a couple of things with my aunt's children, just to see some type of action for the day. I returned from the basement sweating, tired and thirsty from all of that jumping and flipping I was doing, plus my cousin had brought his albino German Shepherd named Sheba out and I was so afraid of her. I walked into the kitchen where my eldest cousin

was at, she was about to wash the dishes and mop the floor.

"Terri, can I please have something to drink?" I asked. She

looked at me and said *"Kimmy, why you so sweaty? What have*

you been doing?" I looked at her and started whining, jumping

up and down, *"Terri... can I please have something to drink,*

I'm about to die from thirst!" She looked at me and said,

"Okay, but don't tell nobody I gave you this!" I looked at her

with my eyes wide and said, *"Okay, I promise!"* My cousin

went to the refrigerator, grabbed a pitcher of *Kool-Aid* and

poured me a jar. The reason why I said jar, is because they

didn't have any real cups or glasses only jars. As I sat there

drinking my *Kool-Aid,* My aunt hollered from the back yard

saying, *"Terri, I hope your cleaning that kitchen! I don't want*

not nan dirty dish in that kitchen, cause' I don't want to hear

your daddy's mouth when he comes in from work! Did you hear

what I said? Clean the kitchen now!" My cousin Terri looked

at me and put her finger up to her lips, signaling me to stay

quiet and replied *"Okay, mama!"* My cousin Terri quickly

called out to one of her brothers to come into the kitchen, while

I continued sitting on the stool at the table drinking my *Kool-Aid*. Suddenly, her brother walked in with an attitude asking, *"What, Terri? What do you want?"* It was very clear that my cousin Garland, was irritated with her. She looked at me, then swiftly turned back to look at him and said, *"Mama said for you to clean this kitchen and I don't want to hear no shit, just clean it!"* He looked at her and shouted, *"YOU'RE A DAMN LIE!"* aggressively. *"She told you to clean it! It's your turn and I'm not cleaning nothing!"* The next thing I know, my cousin *Terri* started hitting him as hard as she could without warning . While in mid swing, cousin Terri demanded her brother to clean that kitchen and wash those dishes but he wasn't taking her crap and began fighting back. While all of this was going on, I continued sitting there calmly, drinking my *Kool-Aid* and watching the fight. I had the best seat in the house. My cousins were fighting for what seemed like hours, even though it really was a few minutes. Their bout was very exciting and one of the best matches I'd ever seen. They were rolling around on that kitchen floor, punching, biting, kicking and scratching until they got tired. After the first round was done, my cousin Terri turned to me with bated breath and said *"Kimmy, you count to three and then we gone start fighting again and you pick the winner!"* I stared at her as I was in full motion to the refrigerator to grab the pitcher of *Kool-Aid*, all while looking her in the eye to see what her reaction would be of me getting more of it. I climbed up on the stool, turned around and said, *"Okay, I'm about to start counting so get ready! 1... 2... 3 Go!"* My cousin Garland immediately started winning. I couldn't help but laugh very hard and loud, the second round had become very entertaining. I sat there drinking my *Kool-Aid* and cheering them on, *that was until I heard my aunt coming through the backdoor*. I instantly jumped off of the stool and ran to my aunt's side, as if I had just walked in on them fighting. *"They fighting and I'm so scared."* I shouted, pretending to cry. My aunt swiftly picked me up and said. *"I know y'all not fighting in front of this baby! Hell, I KNOW Y'ALL NOT FIGHTING AT ALL!"* She shouted, *"TERRI, CLEAN THIS DAMN KITCHEN UP LIKE I SAID AND YOU GET YOUR ASS OUT OF HERE!"* My cousin Garland pushed Terri out of the way and went out the front door. She then looked at me, bald her fist up while silently moving her lips threateningly and said, *"This is not over! I'm going to get you!"* I stuck my tongue out at her and laid my head on my aunt's shoulder as she carried me out the back door to my mom. *"Auntie Mattie, I was so scared."* I said, my aunt Mattie patted me on the back and replied, *"I know baby, I know."* I didn't care what she said or what she did, I was not going to get in any trouble because they decided to fight. Aunt Mattie never knew how long that fight had been going on.

I sat in the backyard with my mom and aunt until I felt that my cousin had left the kitchen. Then I went back into the house to find her youngest daughter Gina but I couldn't find her anywhere. I ran through the house calling out for Gina, when suddenly, her brother jumped from behind the door with his eye lids turned inside out and scared me. I starting screaming and ran as fast as I could as he chased me out of the front door, that's where I saw Gina. She was sitting on the front porch with some of her friends and her brother Règ. I was still in a panic from my goofy cousin scaring me but that didn't stop them from teasing me. My cousin Règ looked at me and said, *"Kim, here comes your boyfriend Boogaloo to give you a kiss and he wore that pink dress just for you!"* I instantly started screaming and crying again, *"Nu'Un! I don't like him, he wants to be a girl! You better get away from me Boogaloo or else I'm going to kill you, cause' you got on a dress like a girl, you must be a sissy! I'm telling on you Règ!"* I cried. Back then, I didn't realize the struggle that Boogaloo was going through. He only had that dress on because he didn't have anything else to wear and I couldn't understand why that's all he had. I quickly ran to the side of the house where I saw my cousin Gina sitting in a broken basement window, well it was more like a cellar because you couldn't enter it from the house and the only way that you could enter was through the outside door in back of the house. My cousin Gina was sitting in that broken out window fearlessly. She was one of those kids who thought she knew everything and I couldn't stand her for that. She always made up stories trying to scare me, I knew that she was planning on doing this by the way she was positioned in that window. *"Kim, the man that lives in this house... is a killer! He* got a big ax and he killed all of the neighborhood kids!" She stated eerily. I looked at her with my hands on my hips and said, *"You're a damn lie! How in the hell did he kill all the kids and y'all still alive? 'Cause last I knew, y'all was all kids except for your mama and daddy!"* Gina looked at me and said, *"I don't really care if you don't believe me, you better stay away or I'm going to have him kill you and your whole generation including you!"* I looked at her and swiftly replied saying, *"For your funky information, you are my generation dummy!"* Gina turned back to me and said aggressively, *"No, I'm not! I don't even like you! I would never be a part of your generation and anyway, you not no kin to me! They found you in the alley!"* I stared at her with my hands on my hips and shouted, *"You a lie, you a fly, you got dookie in your eye, you got 15 babies by the FBI, 5 black, 5 blue, 5 stink like you and everybody in your whole generation, is a lie and if you don't stop lying... I'm going to punch your ass straight through that damn window and then the killer gone kill you and your whole funky entire family! Keep on talking to me, STUPID ASS!"* Gina looked at me daringly and said, *"I'm going to tell that you keep cussing and you ain't gone do nothing to me!"* I looked at her and confidently said, *"Yes, I will!"* Gina then looked at me and said, *"I dare you, 'cause you ain't gone do nothing to me!"* Things were beginning to get out of hand but I tried to warn her, she just wouldn't listen. I began to pace back and forth on the side of that house. I was ready for a fight with my fists balled up, as my cheeks began to inhale and exhale rapidly releasing air. *"Gina... Gina please, please, please don't dare me, cause' I will kill you like a bug! I could care less and you know I'll do it anyway!"* I shouted. Gina stared me down with confidence, as she tried getting up out of that window and said, *"Well if that's the case, I triple dare you!"* I couldn't believe what I was hearing. *Now, why would she do that? You don't triple dare a child that's readily prepared to strike, welcoming whatever repercussions that would follow. That was a huge mistake!* So, I replied with confidence *"Oh, Yeah?"* then I pushed her ass right threw that damn window, never thinking twice about it. For all I knew, she was dead and all I could say as I walked away was, *"Her ass shouldn't have dared me! She'll know the next time!"* I must say, it was cold blooded how I'd walked to the backyard and sat on my

mother's lap. I felt that I was being rewarded for taking Gina

out, wasn't a worry in mind. My mother gave me a barbecued

hot dog, a *Faygo Red Pop*, I'd even ate a burger and waited on

some of the best ribs this side of heaven, all while listening to

Denise LaSalle's "Trapped By This Thing Called Love" as it

played loudly on the radio, all while Gina laid dying in the

basement. I was just carelessly enjoying the festivities, I even

started singing along to the song, *"♫♪Ooh baby!♫♪"* I had it

made until my aunt curiously asked about my cousin, *"Lemma,*

where is Gina?" I looked at her and lied straight to her face, as

I continued eating my hot dog with my lips red from the pop

I'd been drinking and my fingers sticky from the bbq sauce. *"I*

don't know, I haven't seen her all day!" Lying through my

teeth, *knowing good and damn well I had pushed her through*

that window for lying to me. My mom and aunt continued

listening to the music on the radio when all of a sudden, they

heard light crying and whimpering. My aunt looked at my

mom as she was turning the meat and said, *"What was that?*

Did you hear that Annie?" My mother stepped away from the grill, turned the radio down, turned around and began pointing saying, *"Yes, I think it's coming from over there."* Aunt Mattie quickly ran over to the fence that separated the two yards and in a panic, started screaming my cousin's name. *"GINA, GINA?"* She quickly jumped the fence and listened at the cellar door and shouted, *"IT'S COMING FROM HERE ANNIE!"* My Aunt forcibly grabbed that door and began pulling it vigorously. I ran and grabbed onto my mother, scared of what they might find or if Gina would actually be alive to tell that I was the one who pushed her through the window. *She shouldn't have ever been sitting in that window, in the first damn place*! Aunt Mattie was unable to open that cellar door, so she grabbed a crowbar and like Steve Austin, *for all of you who don't know who I am talking about, I'm speaking of the Bionic Man.* She finally broke the padlock and chain off of that shed door and there was Gina, shaking and crying profusely. Gina, staggering her words as she cried uncontrollably said, *"That man was in the basement sharpening his ax to kill me! Mama, he had lots of dead bodies in that basement too and baby dolls,*

177

mama!" My cousin Gina was very shook up, I was just glad she didn't tell on me. It took a lot of years for me to feel remorse behind my actions. She should've listened but as I got older, I did apologize to her. Gina never told on me for pushing her through the window that day and I'm very apologetic and thankful to her for that.

CHAPTER 7

THE NEW SCHOOL

"From Palmer to Schultz"

I t was Labor Day and this meant summer was just about over. The time to go back to school was dawning on us and to celebrate this monumental occasion, my mom and aunt decided to roast a pig for the holiday. They invited everyone over for this special day. What I couldn't believe was, there was this entire pig twirling around in her backyard over an open pit like a rotisserie chicken. I came to learn, that this was one of their many traditions that they'd brought with them from Georgia. I was having a good time playing and running around with all of the other children, until my uncle's nephew Wayne came over and wouldn't leave me alone. He was almost my parents age, saying that he liked me and wanted me to be his girlfriend. I was in elementary school but that didn't stop him from trying his hand. This made me very uncomfortable, I couldn't even play anymore because of it. What could've been just a great family barbecue, was quickly turning into a problem. I had no other choice but to stay close to my parents, this alerted my dad because I was very uneasy. He noticed how I wasn't playing with the others and hanging around the adults. *"Kimberly, baby why aren't you playing with the other kids?"* He asked. I was a bit hesitant at first to tell him what was going on but I did anyway. I looked at my dad and said, *"Cause' that man won't leave me alone, he keeps trying to get me to come with him in the house!"* My dad jumped up out of his seat and said, *"What? Show that Nigga to me!"* Normally, I never wanted to be around my father but this particular night, I was afraid of what that man would do to me. I grabbed my dad by the hand and pulled him toward the front of the house and pointed Wayne out. *"That's him right there!"* My dad walked up to him and said, *"My man, this is my daughter and I better not see you talking to her, looking at her or touching her! I better not even think that you're thinking about her or else, I will kill you! You understand? This is mines! You touch her, you*

touch me!" My dad then aggressively grabbed Wayne by the

collar and my aunt and uncle instantly ran from the backyard.

"What's going on?" Aunt Mattie asked with concern. My mom

then came running screaming my dad's name, *"John, what's*

going on? Let him go, that's Glover's nephew!" She said. My

aunt Mattie then pleaded with my dad to cease the commotion,

"John please let him go and tell us what's going on!" My dad

held Wayne tightly by his collar and said, *"This Nigga messin'*

wit' my daughter and don't nobody mess wit mines! You

understand, I'll kill a Nigga about mine!" Aunt Mattie stared at

him and said, *"Okay, John let him go! Wayne you need to*

leave, cause' you can't come over here messing with these

kids!" Wayne looked at my aunt and said in a soft voice, *"Aunt*

Mattie, I was just playing with her. I didn't mean any harm, I'll

leave her alone but please don't make me leave." My daddy

looked at me while my mother grabbed hold of his arm and

started pulling him back into the backyard, the look on his face

said a lot. *"Come here baby. If that man or any other man*

bothers you, you come and tell yo daddy okay. Now, go and

play!" I gave my daddy a hug and ran off. I didn't have to worry about him anymore but my day was ruined from how uncomfortable I'd felt and after that, I wanted to go home.

The holiday was over and school was beginning that Monday yet I felt no differently about this school, then I had felt about the previous one. I didn't want to go and that was the bottom line. This feeling was nothing new or random, just the truth. I hated school with a passion and I felt that school hated me even more, not to mention I was friendless. With this being a new school and all, it was going to take a whole lot of time to get use to those unfamiliar faces. We were still very new to the neighborhood and unlike the North End, there wasn't many faces that looked like mine. During those times, the Westside was predominantly white and that's exactly what I saw, a lot of white people. Although, I didn't have any friends yet, there were kids on our block. It still wasn't like it was on the North End though and I must admit, there was three girls on the block that became my friends. There was Pebbles, whose grandmother lived across the street from me. Kimberlee lived a block away and her mother had a sports car. I thought that was so cool, it was far different from the Cadillacs I was used to seeing on the North End. Then there was Lynn, who happened to be white and someone that I kind of idolized. Lynn was someone I wanted to be like, look like, have eyes like and even have hair like. She also had an earthy sister named Chrissy, who was a flower child or hippie. She thought everything was cool, hip and peaceful. I remember she would make us lay on the grass and describe the colors and shapes of the clouds. The reason I idolized and wanted to be like Lynn so much had a lot to do with what was subconsciously implanted in my mind from my grandmother. White ice was colder and the grass seemed greener on the other side to her. Lynn was very, very nice to me, even though I was very mean to her on occasions. I can honestly say that she was wonderful *yet* frail. Lynn was my friend and her family loved that she had a friend to play with. Even though Lynn was a very sickly child with a serious heart condition, she didn't allow that to hinder her from enjoying her friendships. As time goes on, I realize more and more that the way I treated her, was my way of lashing out from the treatment I'd received from the children and the teachers at the new school. They were white and she was white, that was the dominant standard back then. Looking back, I realize this hindered me socially and prevented me from experiencing many valuable relationships in life. My sisters didn't demonstrate this same hindrance, they had many friends and didn't ever have trouble making them. It seemed as if everyone they came in contact with liked them a lot.

The first day of school came and my mom registered me at Schulze Elementary school. Once registration was over, she walked with the school's administrator to the classroom that I would soon be a part of. It was official now, school was in session. As the weeks passed, I continued to hate school more and more. Nothing changed but the area I lived in and the school. I'd been there for awhile now, I wasn't the new kid anymore and still, I had no friends. I wasn't learning anything because I was too afraid to raise my hand or answer any questions and not to mention, I was afraid of this girl in my class by the name of Danielle. *I know you're probably wondering how this could've happened. How could the girl who was prepared to blow up the world, cannibalize Timothy and pushed her cousin through a basement window, be afraid of anybody?* Danielle was much smaller than I was *yet* she always managed to find a way to make me cry. She constantly picked on me but she wouldn't be the only one. Now, I know I've done things in my youth that could be looked at as a form of bullying but I never just did those things just because, I was a victim of a cycle that I didn't create. After being tormented by Danielle on a daily basis, I would soon have to face the worse bully in our class... Beatrice. She was the ultimate class bully, big and burley like a lumberjack. *Oh yeah, it gets worse!* I was so terrified of her that I was afraid to tell my parents that she was bothering me. Beatrice was like a grown man compared to me and she demonstrated her force on a daily basis. She always took my lunch money, made me bring her things from home and even had me convincing my mother to purchase things that I didn't really like, just so that I could give them to her. I would lie to my mother's face, pretending I just had to have something or liked certain things, when in reality it was all for Beatrice. She was ruthless and if I didn't have what she'd asked for, it would be off with my head. I couldn't get away from her, she tormented me just that much. The only time that I was finally able to break away from Beatrice, was when I came down with the measles. I'd played sick so much because I was scared to death of her. I was sent to the office on a daily bases claiming to be sick just so that I could avoid seeing or having to deal with Beatrice, but this particular time I was sick. On that particular morning, I explained to my mother that I was very sick before she sent me to school. *"Mommy, I'm sick. I really don't feel good."* My mom looked at me and said, *"Well, you've missed too much school. You can go today and if you still don't feel any better, I'll take you to the doctor when you get out of school."* I looked at her with tears in my eyes and replied *"Okay, mommy but I really don't feel so good."* I felt faint and started to feel like I was going to combust into flames, so I walked to the kitchen and opened the freezer and placed my head on the ice tray. I was very hot and didn't feel good at all.

I left for school that morning and as soon as I got there, I was sent to the office *yet* again. I had thrown up clear fluids the entire morning and wasn't getting any better. The school secretary called my mom saying, *"Ms. Wade, this is Schulze Elementary school calling. Your daughter Kimberly is in the office. She says she is not feeling well, would you like to speak with her?"* Mom was quiet at first on the phone but then she agreed to speak with me. *"Yes, please let me speak with her... Kimberly, what's wrong?"* She asked, I felt very weak and I needed to get out of that place. *"Mommy, I don't feel well! I can't stop throwing up. I need to come home!"* I cried. My mother then said, *"Okay wait until lunch time and then walk home. In the meantime, they will give you some graham crackers and milk to see if that makes you feel a little better."* My mother hung up the phone and the secretary gave me a carton of milk and some graham crackers that I refused to eat. I laid on the office bench until lunch time came, then I went to get my coat and my books and proceeded to leave the school. As I was walking away, someone ran up behind me and pushed me in my back really hard, causing me to fall down. It was Beatrice and despite the fact that I was extremely sick, that didn't stop her from bullying me. I got up and ran out of the school crying all the way home. I even got chased by a dog on the way, this day was definitely a horrible one. By the time I made it home, my mom took one look at me, went and got the thermometer out of the cabinet, took my temperature and informed my grandmother that she had to take me to the emergency room immediately.

When we returned from the emergency room, my mom went into the kitchen and spoke with my grandmother. *"Mama, this girl was really sick."* My grandmother looked at my mother and said, *"What did they say?"* My mom replied saying, *"Well, they said she has the measles but she is not in the contagious stage any longer."* My grandmother got up out of her chair and said, *"Well, you keep her away from the other kids. When will she be alright to go back to school?"* My mom looked at my grandmother and said, *"Well, it might be a couple of months. The doctor will give the go ahead for her to go back to* school." My grandmother lit her cigarette and said, *"Well, I be damned! Contact the school and let the teachers know, so that when she is feeling better, they can have some extra credit work for her to do so she won't be left behind."* I was officially sick and out of school. Despite the circumstances, I was happy to be out and not at school being picked on. For the majority of the time that I was out, I just sat at home watching TV. I got the chance to look at soap operas and shows like *Kelly and Company*, *The Polka Dot Door*, *Rita Bell Prize Movie*, *The Brady Bunch* and *Family Affair*. Even though I was sick, I really enjoyed being home with my mother.

The day came for the doctor to decide if I was well enough to go back to school and according to him, I was. He gave the go ahead for me to go back, *I'd wished he hadn't*. My first day back I was late but it wasn't because of anything that my parents had done, it was because I didn't want to go back. Of course, I gave my mother every excuse on why I shouldn't go to school and why it would be best for me to stay home with her. She didn't buy any of my excuses. I had been playing this game for a long time and the games that had some success once before, didn't work anymore. Now, I would have to go to school every day because of how long I'd been out. This would be a trying time for me to return to a school, that I hated and resented for how horrible I was treated. Well, needless to say I continued to be bullied by Beatrice and *whomever* else felt the need to pick on me.

The day that I went back to school and walked into my class, I was confronted with a pop quiz about the United States. I was given a blank map of America and I was told to label all of the different states. I was puzzled, very lost and didn't understand why I was receiving this quiz. In every last one of my classes, I was hit with a test or a pop quiz at random. I thought that, with me being out of school for several months with a serious illness, would actually exempt me from having to do any of that. I was supposed to get a make up work, along with extra credit, so that I could catch up from being gone so long. Unfortunately, they did not care to give me any make up work, extra credit work or any other assignment to help me catch up.

They enjoyed capitalizing on my miseducation and didn't give a *damn* about this little black child being sick. *It was just another sad blues song to them.* The teacher passed the tests out to the class and my eyes began to deceive me, everything looked like a foreign language. I looked around the class to see what everyone was doing or if they looked as lost as I was, none of that seemed to matter once I heard. *"Now settle down class and put everything away!"* If the look of confusion had a name, it would have been Kimberly. I looked down at the paper and everything seemed to merge together but of course I wasn't going to be allowed to go home, I'd just come back to school from being out for months. *"Let's Begin!"* Stated the teacher with urgency. I continued to look at that test and whispered to myself, *"No one ever taught me this!"* That's when Mrs. Lebow walked past and abruptly slammed her ruler on my desk and shouted, *"NO TALKING!"* I continued looking at the paper and began to whisper to myself again, this time in a panic. *I never knew that there were twelve months in a year, all I knew was that there were holidays that kept me out of school and that was Easter, Thanksgiving and Christmas. Of course, I knew about Summer Vacation and my birthday.* That was the just of it, I was lost. I'd be damned to hell, if anyone had ever taught me where the placements of the different states were and how to locate them on a map. The test was finally over and Mrs. Lebow said, *"Pass your test to the front of the class!"* That's exactly what I did, *however*, the only thing that I could write that I knew for sure, as well as where to place, was my name and the date. *"Did you finish the test that I have given you? Because if you did not, you will not be going to lunch and you will not be going on the playground for recess!"* Stated Mrs. Lebow with agitation. All I could do was look down at the ground, I hadn't finished that test because I didn't know. I wasn't brought up to speed *nor* was I given any sort of make up work to prepare me to be quizzed on. *"Are you dumb or do I need to put a hat on your head that says dunce, to tell everyone just how dumb you really are?"* Stated Mrs. Lebow aggressively, before continuing to punish and degrade me. *"Hold out your hand!"* She shouted while bending my fingers back and began to paddle me, all because I did not know the twelve months of the year or where to place the names of the various states on the map. I instantly flashed back to the last time I was paddled, during the Timothy incident at my last school a couple of years ago. *Yeah, it's levels to this shit!* After paddling me, Mrs. Lebow said, *"I don't know why you people were even allowed to go to school! Your kind is too dumb to learn!"* Mrs. Lebow then pushed me so hard I fell to the ground, triggering her to grab me up by my sweater and make me stand in the corner with my arms up for the remainder of the afternoon. She then vindictively waited for the other children to return from lunch to see me standing in the corner with my hands held high above my head like the letter *"I"* for ignorant, to humiliate and embarrass me. After a while, she finally allowed me to sit at the desk and do the handwriting lesson that she had assigned the class and because I wrote my letters too big, she tore up every hand writing assignment that I had completed. *"Your hand writing is horrific and you don't hold the pencil correctly! You will not be joining the class today or in the near future for a break because you are illiterate!"* I didn't even know what illiterate meant but I knew that I could never ask her the meaning of it, my mom would just have to tell me. Mrs. Lebow allowed the class to go out on the playground and kept me in, given me *yet* another paddle for reasons I am unsure of. She made me return back to the corner with arms up, until it was time to go home. This treatment went on for the duration of my time in her class, she enjoyed abusing me. I learned absolutely nothing while being in her class and she was very proud of that. Her ideology was that no black person or black people as a whole, should have ever been allowed to attend school, especially white schools. Mrs. Lebow was a devout racist and showcased this to all of her black students. Everything she had stated to me, is exactly how I began to think. My self esteem was shattered, I thought that I was dumb and couldn't learn even though my mother made us go to the library, the museums and she taught us a lot yet I was too afraid to let anyone see how smart I was or could be. I'd begun to play dumb because she said I was and maybe just maybe, her words had some truth to them. I was starting to feel this same way about all of my teachers, *maybe I was dumb and was unable to learn.* Mrs. Lebow's prejudice ways diminished the growth of my character from the way I was treated by her and because of how she talked to me. It was of no concern to her of my situation, she didn't care that I had just returned to school from a serious illness. It was her responsibility as my teacher to provide the extra credit work that *per* conversation with my mother and the school administrator, she agreed to do. All she did was paddle, demean and reduce me to my lowest self. Those white teachers never tried to help me and this resulted in a conference with them telling my mother, that they were going to hold me back a grade because I was unable to keep up with the other kids in the class. I'd fallen too far behind and that I would have to attend summer school in order to be placed in my correct grade. They were railroading me into a downward spiral and I didn't have any way to avoid it. Unaware of how this school and its white teachers were treating me, my mother agreed with there plan of action. I swear, I vowed to never ever go back to that school again but that choice was certainly not mines to make. Due to those very malicious words from the infamous Mrs. Lebow, I happen to flunk each and every class that I had. She spoke death to me and my education, I let that into my spirit and the outcome was being left behind. Not only was I left behind, Beatrice was still there and I continued to get bullied on a daily basis.

I became older and was use to changing classes, this was a normal process to me *yet* I still didn't have any friends. Our day would start off in homeroom with bell-work then science, music, the library, gym and math. After that, we'd return to our homeroom. When it came down to my academic classes, I couldn't learn anything and I can't remember anything that I was supposed to or should have learned. I now know that, this was caused from the treatment that I'd received from my white teachers and those children that continued to torment me. I was just not the one to have any interest in school at all. Those white teachers really inflicted chaos into my young mind and made me resent their very existence. Even though most of those teachers were cruel and evil towards me, there was one teacher that I can honestly say helped me and that was my music teacher. She was one of the very few black teachers that I had. Even though she was strict and I did get a couple of light paddled licks in her classroom as well, I can honestly convey to you that she believed in me more than I believed in my self and what I was capable of doing. Mrs. Parish was her name and although she was Dr. Parish, she allowed us to call her Mrs. Parish. She was an amazing teacher or shall I say, Dr. of Music. I learned everything about music and how to appreciate the arts in her class. Despite not remembering much of anything in my other classes, I still remember everything she taught me. Mrs. Parish understood the importance of inspiring and up lifting the children of her race. Before we began work in her class, we would have to recite the black national anthem, *"Lift Every Voice and Sing."* Even though I loved her class, I didn't fully appreciate it back then because of how I felt inside but I appreciate it now. I appreciate what she was doing from the songs we had to sing, to the poems we had to recite. She educed me the best way she knew how to, *which is a hell of a lot more than I can say about those other teachers*. Mrs. Parish taught me a lot but the one thing that stands out in my mind is a poem I had to learn. The poem was written by the poet Robert Frost, it resonated with everything I was going through during that time. *"Stopping by the Woods on a Snowy Evening"* was the title and the artistically rhythmic style of teaching Mrs. Parish taught us in, helped me to learn tremendously in her class. She made everything interesting, wonderful, valuable and she taught us everything in the form of a song, even the poems. I looked forward to going to her class every day. Mrs. Parish would call us up to her desk one by one and make us whisper the poems she had taught us in her ear, this was done so that she would be aware of the children who were learning and who needed extra help. I was so eager and couldn't wait for her to call on me to come to her desk to whisper the poem in her ear, this made me feel overjoyed. *"Kimberly, please come up to my desk. Do you remember the poem I taught you?"* Said Mrs. Parish. I looked at her eagerly, with a smile on my face and said, *"Yes, I do!"* She looked at me with a smile on her face and said, *"Come a little closer and let's hear it!"* I stepped closer and recited the poem that she'd taught me in her ear.

"Stopping by the Woods on a Snowy Evening" by

Robert Frost.

"Whose woods these are I think I know. His house is

in the village though. He will not see me stopping

here.

To watch his Wood's fill up with snow. My little Horse

must think it queer. To stop without a farm house

near.

Between the woods and frozen Lake. The darkest

evening of the year. He gives his harness bells a

shake. To ask if there is some mistake.

The only other sound's, the sweep of easy wind and

downy flake. The Woods are lovely dark and deep.

But I have promises to keep. And miles to go before

I sleep, and miles to go before I sleep." (frost, 1923),

Mrs. Parish looked at me, as if I'd just made her soul light up

and said with excitement, *"Very good!"* I thought that poem

was so beautiful. The class would have to recite a different poem at the beginning of every class and then after lunch, we would come back to class and sing the very poem that we had to recite at the beginning of class. Mrs. Parish understood the essence of music and its origins. How it moved and inspired the people and most importantly, the children. When it came to her style of teaching, she embraced the perfect formula of how music can be used to heal her students, *especially her black students*. In her eyes, it was us who held the keys of freedom, being children of rhythm and love we could create a brighter day.

Even though I was left behind, I am happy to say that I received an *"A"* in her class... but I managed to fail everything else. This was an awful situation for me and because of this reason alone, I began skipping school. I couldn't handle the constant teasing and ridicule of my classmates because of my failure to pass to the next grade level. See, school was horrible in my eyes and I felt as if none of my teachers liked me *nor* did the other kids like me. I was very shy, I had no social skills because of how I was raised and I never had to deal with anyone outside of my family on this level. I was never taught how to adapt in society. So, of course there was no promotion for me. *Do you know what serious ramifications this has on a child?* I mean, I was not held back because I couldn't learn, I was sick and was quarantined from school, otherwise I would have been there and would have been on pace. This was awful and of course my mother sent me to summer school, *which*, I was under the impression that I would be placed in my right grade after summer vacation. That didn't happen and this really made me hate school even more, not to mention I was still being bullied by Beatrice. I hated school and all that it was about. The school system failed me and I am sure that they failed and are still failing, a host of other children because they are afraid to ask questions, raise their hands or because there ashamed of the way they dress. You never know the issues that many children face. It is my belief that a good portion of these teachers don't care or give a *damn*. I know the majority of the ones that I had didn't, they were just there for a pay check and not to help the black children to succeed. The majority of the children that were in my class were white, with the exception of me and Danielle. However, she had been there since kindergarten, had many friends and even though she was black, she didn't always act like it. The teacher didn't like her either and would get angry if she seen the white children playing with her. Now, don't get me wrong, I am not a racist person at all but you have to remember that this was a time in society when there was a lot of racial tension. This is post civil rights, so you still had schools that were segregated but a lot of neighborhoods were not and everyone was not treated equal. I received some of the most horrific examples of racism by the hands of those white teachers at that school, there sole purpose was to try and diminish the people of my culture. A people who'd taught them how to think, invent, build empires and civilizations, even though they remain uncivilized at times. Those people, who they said shouldn't be allowed to attend school and should remain within the belch of high society. A people who they've tried to emulate, imitate and humiliate under the guise supremacy. Please tell me, *how can a people be of no value or worth to you, when from their ancestors you received all of your value, knowledge and worth?* You only steal what you cannot afford to have and since they were unable to do what my ancestors did, they stole everything about us. I now understand that my people have been the misrepresented piece of the larger spectrum.

SKIPPING SCHOOL

On a cold and rainy day in November, I decided that I was never going back to school again. There would be no more getting chased home from school, being told that I was going to get my butt kicked at the end of the day and there definitely wouldn't be anymore of me giving my lunch money up or lunch away. I would be free from all of that, I was done. I'd come up with a brilliant plan because acting sick and faking throwing up on the way to school was not working anymore *nor* was pulling out the old guns and hiding one shoe, I had to do something new. I was being nosey and listening to my sister Kelly and my aunt

Debra, stating how they had ditched school and how much fun

it was, so I decided that I would ditch or skip school also. I was

at least going to try it and see how that would work out for me.

I thought to myself as I sat at the kitchen table eating breakfast,

that it was either I skip school or face Beatrice. Her bullying

had reached the point of torture by this time and I could no

longer bare it. So, my plan was to leave home a little later than

usual and go over to my aunt Dorothy's house, who lived two

blocks down and across the field from where we lived. I would

wait for her and my uncle to leave for work, then I'd sneak and

sit in their old car that wasn't being used. I followed through

with this plan, even though I was very nervous on the first day,

skipping school became easier and easier as the days went bye.

I would sit in that old car in their backyard for hours, without

any care of ever going back to school. I would sit there until I

thought school was over, which seemed like a lifetime to me. I

would go home once I seen the other children walking, acting

as if I had been in school all day. My aunt and uncle were

always at work so, *who would be the wiser?* No one would

ever know that I was skipping school in that green Ford LTD.

That car had been sitting there for many years, nestled up in

their driveway. I was able to get away with this for almost three

weeks, it never dawned on me the repercussions of what I'd do

if I were to ever get caught. I just had to get away from

Beatrice. I would eat my lunch, read my books and then fall

asleep. Before you knew it, a full day of school had passed.

Those three weeks seemed endless, I didn't even recognize

their old nosy neighbor Mrs. Jaquay, who had been watching

me all along. She'd seen me come and going for about a week,

before she revealed her intentions of telling my aunt and uncle

that I'd been frequently coming over early in the morning,

staying in their car until school was out. *Why didn't she mind*

her own damn business, was just beyond me. Actually, she

should have said something when she first saw me doing this,

not that it would have mattered to me one bit. I still continued

to skip school in that car. Understand, I would have rather been

in trouble with my aunt and uncle, than having to face the

bullying that was going on at that school. So, I continued to

skip and I would deal with the consequences of my actions

later. I'd skipped so much school at this point, I became bored and lonely. Sitting there for all of those hours, without any sort of entertainment and for many days out of the week, was very depressing and I for *damn* sure didn't have any friends to accompany me. So to make things more interesting, I decided to bring one of my little sisters and her friend along with me. I know what you're thinking, "*Why make matters worse?*" *Don't judge me, I was young and didn't know what else to do.* At first, they were very reluctant to come along but had decided with a little convincing from me, that they would come. I wasn't that much older *yet* I had a tremendous influence on what they did and how they thought. I was walking them to school, so they had to do what I told them to do. However, thinking back in hindsight, I should have never taken them with me. The both of them cried the majority of the time, not to mention they didn't want to sit in the car, they wanted to play and run around outside in the backyard, which to me was not a safe thing to do. This would definitely get me caught and all because I would not let them do what they wanted to do, they formed a mutiny against me, decided they didn't want to stay and wanted to go home. *"We want to go home right now! Yeah, we want to go home!"* They shouted repeatedly. I looked at them both seriously and said, *"I am the oldest and I say when we go, cause' we can't go right now. I don't see anybody walking home from school!"* They both looked at me and replied *"okay"* and continued to play in the back seat of the car. This was working out fine until Mrs. Jaquay came outside. She walked up the driveway to the car and started to bam on the window, hitting the glass repeatedly. She startled me and then yelled for us to leave. *"Get out of there! Did you hear me? Get out of the car right now! You know you ain't got no business in this car in the first place! It's too dangerous and I already called your auntie and uncle and they will deal with you later but in the meantime, GET OUT NOW AND GO HOME!"* We got out of the car and began to walk down the street when suddenly it began to rain, this was all I needed. I was not aware of what time it was, so how could I go home and take them with me. *Damn, this is just some bad luck!* We continued to walk, for what seemed like many miles but in actuality, we were just two blocks away from our house. To avoid going home, I decided to go in a different direction. At first I thought, maybe we can go up to the school and wait around until the bell rings. I scrapped that plan once I started to worry about if we'd be spotted by the principal, so that wouldn't work. It was still too early for us to be out of school, we still had about an hour or hour and a half left. *"This is some bull crap! If it weren't for that nosey Mrs. Jaquay and her making us leave, we could have still been there dry and out of the rain but no! This is why we had to leave earlier than anticipated!"* I'd thought out loud, as we continued walking through the rain. The more we walked, the more I began to panic. I couldn't go home, I couldn't go to school either and not to mention, it was still too early. I started to scream and cry because I was wet and cold, I was out of ideas and I didn't know what to do or where to go. It would have been very different, if I'd been alone but I had my little sister and her friend with me. As we walked through the wilderness of this unfamiliar street, my many cries triggered the girls to start crying, *"We're, going to tell on you, cause' you didn't take us to school and we cold!"* I looked at them both and shouted, *"Shut up all that crying! We are about to go to school right now!"* I figured if I went up to the school, the girls couldn't tell on me and say they were never at school and *who would believe Mrs. Jaquay? She was an old senile liar, how could she prove that she saw me today or any other day for that matter?* It was her word against mines and she could never prove that she saw me, because then the tables would turn on her. *"Why would you let them stay in that car or her for that matter?"* is what they would ask her and she wouldn't have the answers or maybe, just maybe they would believe her? *Damn! I forgot to move my trash from the car.* We continued walking in the rain endlessly, hoping that some type of bailout would come. As I continued to think of a lie, just in case Mrs. Jaquay was able to convince my aunt and uncle of what I'd been doing. Who by the way, would most definitely tell my mom of their neighbor spotting me on more than one occasion in that car, in their driveway and that I couldn't have been going to school because I was there every day at the same time. I started focusing on what I could say to my mother but when I thought that I'd finally got close to an explanation, I suddenly see my older sister walking in my direction down the very street I never walk down. Things kept getting worst and as soon as I thought she wouldn't notice me, my sister Shay started yelling. *"I see you Kim! Yeah, that's right! I see you and you already know I'm telling on you!"* Now the gig was definitely up and I knew that I was going to be in a world of trouble once I got home. I knew that no one would listen to the reason why I had to do this thing. So, I decided that I was not going to ever go home and I took off running as fast as I could. I left the girls behind, thinking that someone would come along and help them to get home but as I ran, so did they. I ran even faster, I knew that all they would do was slow me down. *"How can something like this happen?"* I cried, I knew that I had been careful in the past but this time it had to be the girls. If I had not become so lonely and in need of some company, I would've never got caught. My plan had been successful for more than three weeks and I let my guard down. I thought no one would have known what I was doing, I was living fancy free in that Ford LTD, until *Mrs. Nosy Ass* interfered! Now, I was so afraid, more afraid than I'd been. I knew that my sister meant what she said, now I had to worry about two people telling on me. *"I should run away!"* I cried, running faster and faster without reserving the little breath I had left in me. Running towards the same vehicle that had gotten me in this mess in the first *damn* place, I didn't know where else to go. I could have lived in that car, if not for Mrs. Jaquay and sneak in the house when my aunt and uncle left for work. They always kept the back door opened and I could've lived off of the cookies she kept in the green cookie jar, that was near the phone on her counter. She would never know unless Mrs. Jaquay told her. *"Oh man!"* I'd thought. I forgot they had two big German Shepherd dogs, named Tony and Pepper and they would never let me in that house if my aunt and uncle were gone. That idea would never work. As I continued running thru the alley, my main concern was I didn't know how I'd ever explain this to my mother. I already knew that my sister was going to tell her and *MA'MA.* I would have to deal with it, I just couldn't tell them what I was going through. I heard my sister yelling my name and I suddenly felt someone running up behind me. With a pop bottle in my hand, I quickly turned around, swung the bottle and hit whoever it was coming up behind me right in the eye. To my surprise, it wasn't who I thought it would be, it was Carl from down the street. *"I'm telling on you! You could have put his eye out! Come here Carl, I'm telling on you Kim!"* Shouted Shay. I could just tell the truth, I was just scared and he ran up behind me. I panicked and made a mistake and hit him, I didn't mean to do it. *"I'm so sorry, I didn't mean to. Please don't tell on me!"* I cried, begging Carl not to tell as I self examined his eye. My sister Shay looked at him and began shouting, *"Look at his eye, you bust his eye open! He has to tell!"* I was so embarrassed, my mother was going to be so mad at me and she would never go for me hitting anyone especially with a bottle, not to mention I was skipping school. There was just no excuse behind my actions, things quickly went from bad to worse on this day. My mother taught us to be proud in any and everything that we do and that we could accomplish anything and to not run from nothing or anyone. So, *how could she even go for whatever excuse I may have had? "Oh, well!"* I'd thought to myself, as me and my sister walked home slowly. With tears in my eyes, I turned to my sister and remorsefully said, *"I'm sorry Shay! For everything!"* She looked at me and replied with an attitude, *"Sorry didn't do it, you did! So, don't be sorry now, cause' I'm still telling on you!"* My sister Shay couldn't find any sympathy for me *nor* was I able to tell her what was really going on. When we finally made it home and walked through the door, I was very hesitant. Before I could gather myself, the shouting began. *"KIMBERLY, COME HERE RIGHT NOW!"* I couldn't even settle my feet before my mother was calling me and I didn't know what she'd already heard or not, I just knew I was in trouble. I even tried explaining my side of the story and she was buying it until Carl's mother called, saying that she had to take him to the emergency room where they had to put 6 stitches in his eye. *"You could have put that boy's eye out and I'm going to whoop you! Cause' I have to pay for this!"* As my mother continued to discipline me, my mind had become blank and I was beyond done. I didn't care, I was just over everything at this point. Carl was just a casualty of what I had pent up inside. I'd reached a boiling point from enduring such a severe amount of bullying, at the hands of so many, for the last few years at such a consistently high level. Besides, he should've never ran up behind me like he did and Beatrice should have never bullied me. Only in a perfect world, would none of that ever had happened.

The next day came and I went to school as usual. It seemed to be a normal day at first, I went to my classes and wasn't hesitant to do so. Well, this small moment of solace would abruptly come to an end, once lunchtime came around. *"I know you have my lunch money and where are the cupcakes you were supposed to tell your mother to buy?"* Said Beatrice aggressively, while using her normal tactics of intimidation. I was tired of this treatment, especially with what I'd gone through yesterday. I looked at her and said, *"I don't have any of that, I haven't been to school. I'll try to bring you some stuff tomorrow, cause' I have to eat the school lunch today."* Beatrice stared at me with agitation and shouted, *"Hell naw and if you don't have my candy and cupcakes and not to mention, you don't have the money that you're supposed to give me, I'm going to kick your butt after school!"* Beatrice then turned and swiftly walked away. As she was walking, she suddenly stopped and turned back around after a few steps and then balled her right fist up, hitting her left hand while mumbling. *"I'm going to kick your butt after school!"* After threatening me once more, Beatrice finally walked away.

It was now time to go on the playground for recess, needless to say I didn't go. I wanted no parts of being beaten up. The day seemed to go by really fast and before I knew it, the bell rang for us to be dismissed from school. Time sped up tremendously, as if the universe wanted to see how this day would play out. I decided to take a different route home, so that I would not run into Beatrice. However, the kids made that impossible because all I heard was, *"There she is right there, Beatrice! Kim, don't run!"* They shouted continuously, this instantly raised my adrenaline level. I was spotted *yet* again and I could only think to myself, *"How can I run? When all of the kids were surrounding me."* I was trapped, enclosed in a circle with my day one nemesis at this school, as if we were to fight till the death. Me and Beatrice began to walk around each other, *endlessly*. I didn't want to fight. Even though I'd been tormented and tortured by this girl for a few years now, I didn't want any trouble. I know your probably thinking, *"Kim, why didn't you just tell your older sisters or even your mother?"* and I would tell you that, *"I was just too afraid!"* This school had broken my spirit and to be bullied consistently, every single day for the last few years, took the worst toll on my mind. We continued walking around each other and the more I orbited around her, the more I needed to get out of this. I thought I would have a way or some form of refuge but that didn't happen. Someone placed a stick on Beatrice's shoulder, then I heard shouting from the mob of children. *"Knock that stick off her shoulder! Yeah, knock the stick off her shoulder, cause' we gone be here all day!"* The crowd was becoming impatient, they wanted to see blood and mayhem, like we were gladiators in a Roman Coliseum. They continued to shout compulsively, when suddenly, someone pushed me into Beatrice. We instantly began fighting and I went black. I jumped on her and knocked her to the ground! I began choking her out, pulling her hair, punching and scratching her repeatedly. All of the psychological pain and abuse that I'd

216

suffered through because of her and those prejudice teachers, was present in my fists. Someone even tried pulling me off of her and I wasn't having any of that, so I continued punching, biting and kicking her vigorously. There would be no let up, Beatrice had caught these hands and nothing was going to stop me from ending her. Until suddenly, she got away from me shouting and crying, *"I'm telling my sister and brother on you!"* Before I knew it, I grabbed my coat and books and I took off running in the opposite direction. I'd defeated her *yet* I was still very afraid and all I could hear, was faint voices in the distance saying, *"Don't run Kim! Don't run you have sisters too! We're not going to let anyone do anything to you, don't run!"* It was the voices of some of my sister's friends, they were begging me to stop running but I continued to anyway. I vowed to never go back to that school again, I didn't want to face it anymore. I ran all the way home, went into the house and acted as if nothing ever happened.

I woke up for school the next day and tried to act as if I were very sick, I didn't want to see Beatrice. Even though I'd afflicted the same humiliation onto her that she'd did to me, I still couldn't face her. My mother was not having any of that and made me go to school, I would have to face this head on. I arrived at school and was immediately called into the principle's office, *for what?* I didn't have the slightest clue. Once I arrived into the office, to my surprise, I was met by the principal, Beatrice and her mother. According to her, I had been bullying her, she was very afraid of me and that I picked a fight with her on the way home from school. Beatrice lied and turned everything around on me. I tried explaining to them, that I was not the person that was bullying and the one who was actually bullied by her, since I had started going to that school but they were not listening. I had been going to that school for a number of years at that point, so the frustration of being blamed for what I'd never done, was very infuriating. The principal Mr. Allen turned to me and said, *"Kimberly, we can't and will not tolerate bulling, now bend over!"* As I bent over to receive two whacks from his paddle, I began to cry. I was so over this treatment, it all came down to them being against me *yet* again.

Even though I'd won my battle with Beatrice, she was leading the war. I was still afraid of her and all of the others that had teased, pushed, hit and kicked me. Unfortunately, school had to continue for me, *cause'* I was just too young to drop out and my mother would never allow that to happen.

CHAPTER 8

I'M GROWING UP

"I'm not that same naive little girl I used to be."

Summer came back around to greet me *yet* again. I was officially growing up, maturing and adapting to being an older sister. Life on the Westside was changing though, there wasn't as many white folks as it was when we'd first moved here. It seemed as if one day, they just up and flew away in droves. Enquiring minds would like to know why, but that's another story. I was glad to be out of school and ready to enjoy my vacation. I was always doing something recreational with my sisters or cousins, there was always some activity to preoccupy our time. We would go skating, on family trips to amusement parks like *Cedar Point*, the beach and even swimming. I can recall this one day in particular when I, along with my sister and a couple of my cousins, were about to go swimming... *but of course, it didn't go as planned.*

"Let's go Kim! Ugh your funky self didn't even get in the shower yet!" Stated Achy. *"Alright, alright but you better not call me funky no more or else! Let me know if MA'MA or Grace is coming, cause' you already know I'm not supposed to get in this shower. Stupid ass rules! Get out and close the door behind you!"* I shouted while proceeding to get in that *forbidden* shower. Remember how I explained earlier that there were new rules that came along with our new house, well not getting in the shower on the first level was one of them. *"Alright but hurry up or we leaving you! You already know you want to see Brian wit' cho fast butt and I know he's going swimming, all of them are!"* Achy said sarcastically, as she stood outside of the bathroom. *"She get on my nerve! She*

always making us late!" Stated Shay. *"Yep!"* Said my cousin Toria in agreement with her. *"... And you already know, I'm trying to see Marty and Jonathan. We should just leave her."* Shay continued. {*singing coming from the shower*}...*"Wait a minute, did you hear that?"* Shay exclaimed, placing Achy and Toria in a bewilderment. *"Heard what?"* asked Toria before Shay placed her hand over her mouth. *"Shush! Shut up!"* Whispered Shay. {*singing continues from shower*}...*"Oh my God! Do you hear Kim, cussin' up a storm?"* The three of them snuck in the bathroom, eavesdropping and heard me singing loudly with perfect pitch and melody. {*singing continues*}... *"PEANUT BUTTER, MOTHERFUCKA, TWO TIMES BITCH! YOU MESS AROUND WITH ME, YOU'LL GET YOUR ASS KICKED! CAUSE' I DON'T PLAY THAT SHIT, CAUSE' I'M A TI TI TUCKER AND A BAD MOTHERFUCKER!"* Shay quickly pushed the door very hard to startle me, causing it to slam up against the wall abruptly. *"WHAT WAS THAT NOISE!"* Yelled *MA'MA*. *"Ooh, ooh, I caught your butt! I heard everything that you said and I'm telling! So, don't even for one moment think you're going swimming with us!*

222

MA'MA... MA'MA, Kim is in the shower when you told her not to get in there and she is just cussing up a storm! She thinks she's going swimming but I know she ain't going with me saying all of that stuff!" Shouted Shay. My grandmother immediately ran to the bathroom and shouted *"Didn't I tell your ass not to get in that shower? It leaks in the basement! NOW GET YOUR BLACK ASS OUT OF THERE! You're so hard headed, but a hard head makes a soft ass! NOW MAKE HASTE AND GET CHO' ASS OUT OF THIS BATHROOM AND GO UPSTAIRS AND DON'T FOR ONE MOMENT... THINK YOU'RE GOING SWIMMING!"* I was stunned and caught off guard that they bombarded that bathroom. I looked at my grandmother and said *"But I didn't even do nothing! I can't never go nowhere! They always telling!"* MA'MA looked at me and shouted, *"DIDN'T I SAY TAKE YOUR NARROW ASS UPSTAIRS? ... AND DON'T COME BACK DOWN UNTIL I TELL YOU THAT YOU CAN AND I MEAN IT!"* I was furious that they did this to me, they just didn't want me to go swimming with them. I stomped up the stairs, fell out on the bed and started kicking, screaming and crying. *"I can't never go nowhere or do nothing! They always lying on me, I hate*

them! That's okay, cause' I'm going to get every last one of

them back!" I cried, swearing my revenge on them. Suddenly,

my grandmother came to the bottom of the stairs and shouted,

"DIDN'T I TELL YOUR ASS, I DON'T WANT TO HEAR ALL

THAT DAMN CRYING AND FUSSING? NOW SHUT YOUR

MOUTH, BEFORE I GIVE YOU SOMETHING TO CRY

ABOUT!... [puts her cigarette back in her mouth]... These

damn kids get on my last nerve!" My grandmother walked

back into the kitchen and continued preparing dinner for the

evening.

The morning turned into the afternoon and I had fallen asleep. I

was soon awakened by my cousin Achy's voice saying, *"I got*

a new book from my friend. I would let you see it but you

probably can't read cause on your report card it said reading

below grade level!" She laughed. *"I don't want to see your*

stupid book anyway and if I did, I would just take it from you!"

I stated with agitation. *"I wish you would! You won't be taking*

anything from me!" Stated Achy confidently. I stared at her and said, *"Forget you, forgot you!"* before running down the stairs and out of the front door. As I was sitting there, Achy who followed closely behind, approached me with an attitude. *"That's why we told on you and you couldn't come swimming!"* Stated Achy, teasingly. *"Oh really, so it was you? Well, well now I know! Anyway, I didn't want to go with y'all!"* I replied, Achy looked at me and said, *"Well, then you won't care if I told you that Brian was there and he asked about you. We told him you got in trouble and couldn't come and he said so what and bust out laughing at your stupid butt!"* She continued to tease me and I was beyond irritated by this point. *"You better get out of my face and I didn't want to go anyway! I'm not trying to drown and I don't care about that ugly boy anyway!"* I shouted before giving her a warning, *"You need to get out of my face for real Achy, cause I'm not stunting you!"* I didn't want to be bothered but she just kept right on teasing. *"Well, if you really want to see it you can and I'll tell you what Brian really said. Anyway, he probably likes me!"* I stared at Achy, as she stood with her back against the bricks near the front door and replied, *"I know I can see your book if I want too and stop talking to*

225

me! Especially, about Brian big headed butt and if I wanted, I'll take everything you have from you!" Achy looked at me and yelled, *"You won't take nothing from me!"* I got closer to her and said, *"If you dare me, I will take it from you and kill you in the process! You are so stupid, that's why I can't stand you! Why did you come out here anyway? I didn't tell you to follow me, your white butt!"* Achy looked at me and said, *"Say I'm white one more time and I'll show you who's white! My mama and daddy is both black!"* I stood up and got close to Achy's face, as she stood with her back against the bricks. *"YOU JUST THINK YOUR BETTER THAN ME, AND YOU'RE NOT! THAT'S WHY I DON'T LIKE YOU!"* I screamed, I then grabbed Achy and started banging her head up against the brick wall repeatedly. I spazzed out and there was no turning back. Achy began to silently cry with her mouth wide open but no sound dared to escape it. I just knew I was going to be in more trouble now. I was scared, so I immediately tried to think of what I could do to stop Achy from telling MA'MA on me. *"Okay, okay I'm sorry. Just hit me! You can punch me in the stomach."* Achy snatched away from my grip and ran in the house, I instantly started to panic. So, in an attempt to thwart any punishment that would be bestowed onto me, I grabbed my aunt Mary's red lipstick that I'd taken earlier out of my pocket and I began to write *"HELTER SKELTER! I'M GOING TO KILL EVERYBODY IN YOUR HOUSE!"* on the front porch... (*sigh*)... I had seen the *Charles Manson movie* on the television earlier that day, *I didn't know what else to do.*

5 minutes had passed and I was hiding on the side of the porch. *"DAMN ,I GOTTA PEE!"* I yelled. I peered around the corner of the porch and ran to the side door in an attempt to not be heard. I tip toed up the stairs, only to be caught by *MA'MA*. *"I know your black ass didn't write on that porch!"* She stated. *"Achy told me what you did to her. Take your black ass in there and apologize right now! Then come back in here and get this bucket, cause' your ass is about to scrub my porch clean and I mean that. I should beat your ass! What is wrong with you child?"* My grandmother scolded me for what I'd done. If she hadn't teased me and said Brian liked her, I wouldn't have hit her. I walked in the room where Achy was laid out and

227

sarcastically said, *"I'm sorry!"* I then walked out of the room and into the kitchen. I grabbed the bucket, a scrubbing brush and I walked out of the side door. I went to the front of the house, forgetting that I had still had to pee and began scrubbing the porch. In the midst of scrubbing, I started crying. *"I hate all of them!"* I mumbled. They had successfully ruined my day, maybe I'll go swimming some other time.

SQUARE BIZ! I'M GOING SWIMMING!

A few weeks have passed and my cousin Achy and I are back speaking again. It was still the summertime, very hot and we were going swimming. This day was different from the last time, when they foiled my plans of going. I really just wanted to go skating but who would decline going swimming on a hot *ass* day. I most certainly wasn't...

"Are we going swimming today or what?" I'd anxiously asked. *"You know good and well everyone's going to be there including Leonard Vaughn!"* Achy laughed. *"Well, I'm definitely not trying to see his short ugly butt at all and plus, Harold might be with him and he's weird!"* I'd exclaimed, *"Well, whatever we're going to do, we better do it now before MA'MA comes and tells us we can't go!"* I continued. *"Well that's all good and fine if we don't, cause' you know I have the back up plan. The only reason I told my mama I was going swimming, is so I wouldn't have to stay at dance class. I told her you were coming with me, then on the first break we just sneak away, go up to the school then later my daddy is taking us skating!"* Stated Achy. I looked at Achy and said, *"Square Biz?"* Achy looked back at me and said. *"Square Biz!"* I tried to act as if I wasn't excited to go and said in a smug tone, *"Yeah, I guess that's cool but unlike you, I don't have no money*

and no where to get any from. So, you have to walk with me to take these bottles back, cool?" Achy looked at me and said, *"Cool!"* As we were walking to the store, I began to feel a bit jealous of Achy, she was always able to do the things she wanted to do. She had more money to buy things, always had the latest clothes and everybody liked her because of how *light skinned* she was. I didn't have the luxury to do the things she was able to do, because my mother had too many kids. This would take away the funding I'd needed to be able to do extra things. When we got back from the store, My aunt Shaky dropped us off at Achy's dance class. We stayed for about an hour, then we snuck away. *"I hope you got your swimming suit with you Achy! You know what, maybe we shouldn't even go swimming! I just have a bad feeling about today, you probably going to get in trouble like you always do!"* I stated. We both started laughing as we walked up to the school. When we arrived, we headed to the girls locker room to change into our bathing suits. *"You ready?"* asked Achy, *"Yep, let's go!"* I replied.

We went to the pool and jumped in, instantly sparking a great time. As we were playing around splashing in the water, someone suddenly threw our friend Tammy into the deep end unexpectedly. We hadn't even been at the pool for an hour yet, when this event took place. So, we immediately sprung into action. It seemed as if the life guard wasn't paying any attention, now it was left up to me and Achy to rescue her. Achy grabbed Tammy on her left side but Tammy in a panic, began to fight. This rendered Achy helpless, causing her to sink to the bottom of the pool as if she was letting go. I instantly seen this and began to scream out, *"HELP! SOMEBODY HELP THEM!"* I didn't no if anyone heard me, so I swam under the water were Achy was. She was in an upright position as if she was sitting in a chair, looking up to the heavens when I grabbed her and brought her up out of the water. The life guard finally seen what was going on and jumped into the water, picked Tammy up and threw her to the shallow end of the pool and did the same to me and Achy. Even though we didn't need him anymore, I guess he did what he had to do. We climbed out of the pool and I looked at Achy frantically and said. *"I knew it, I had a feeling that something was going to happen! Let's not ever go swimming again!"* Achy then gave me a high five and said. *"I know that's right, I ain't never going swimming again!"* We walked to the locker room, changed clothes and walked out of the school. Me and Achy then locked our arms together and began to dance, singing our way back home to get ready for skating. *{singing and laughing; "♪♪ Chic Chic... Tada da dat do dat... ♪♪ Chic!"}*

Even though me and my cousin Achy have had our share of battles, we still enjoyed our youth together. *I did just save her life, you know? "SQAURE BIZ!"*

CLOSING

THE MAGICAL JACKET

"It was all worth it!"

The time has finally come for me to breakdown, *why* I was running for my life at the beginning of this book. I know it's been a long journey for us all and I'm thankful that you stuck around. While we reminisced back in time, you got a bird's eye view of my childhood, the struggles I'd faced and the many woes I'd endured while growing up in Detroit. You even got a glimpse into my family history and through all of that, you are here to understand me and why I behaved the way I did in my youth. I'm grateful and let's continue.

It was a cold and brisk October day, a little colder than usual. School was in session and my feelings towards it, didn't waver from the way I'd initially felt. *"Kimberly get up and get dressed and get your sisters up after you're done, so that you can eat and won't be late for school... Did you hear me? Get your behind up right now!"* My mother immediately disrupted one of the best slumbers I'd been in. I stretched and wiped the sleep from my eyes, *"Damn."* I whispered. *"Do I have to go to school today? My stomach hurts!"* I cried, (*it didn't really hurt though*). It was no secret, me and school were not friends. I would stop at nothing to never, ever have to go again. I climbed out of the bed with my t-shirt hanging off of my shoulders and my hair standing straight up on my head, I was freezing. *"Momma, it's cold in here, so I know it's extra cold outside! So, do we have to go today?"* I yelled. My mom quickly replied stating, *"Well, you already know there not going to turn the heat up and you're not staying home! So, hurry up and get dressed and then go and stand in front of the vent until I'm finished getting them ready!"* My mother exclaimed, as she continued ironing my little sisters clothes for school. *"What in the hell happened to Indian Summer?"* I'd sarcastically asked myself while getting dressed. After I was done getting myself together I was ready to go. I stared at my sisters who were moving in slow motion while my mother slathered grease on their hair and pressed their edges down. While she searched for barrettes and rubber-bands to put their hair up in ponytails, my patience wore thin. *"Can you please hurry up with their hair? It's time for us to go, we're going to be late!"* I whined, before walking towards the front door. This had to be karma for all the times I made my older sisters late for school, when I was the youngest. I was surely going to leave them but before I could escape, my mom shouted *"Before you take your behind out that door, look over there in that drawer and see if you can find me a couple of rubber-bands!"* I hurried to the drawer and grabbed a hand full of whatever I could find, threw it at her and ran out the door. I wasn't going to be let off the hook that easy, especially for throwing something at my mother. *"Don't you ever throw anything at me again Kimberly! Cause' if you do, I'm going to beat your behind and I mean that!"* However, I paid none of my mother's rants or threats any attention, had she stopped having all of those damn babies after me, there wouldn't be any issues. I stood on the front porch, stretched my arms out, took a deep breath and inhaled the crisp coolness of the morning. It smelled so fresh. I was feeling so good, I even took a bite of my tuna sandwich. *Yep, you heard right! I was still hooked on tuna sandwiches. "Uhm, mmm this is so good! [turns to little sisters] Want some? Well, you can't have none!"* I'd teasingly shouted, while jumping off of the front porch. With one leap, my feet hit the ground and I took off running down the street. *"Wait for us! If you don't, I'm telling on you! You're stupid self!"* cried my little sisters as I quickly evaded them. *"I don't care if you do! Tell, tell go to jail, hang you're britches on a nail! If you cry, I'll pick them up and if you don't, I'll kick your butt! So, go on... tell if you want too! Nobody's going to do anything to me, plus I'm the one who always walks you to school dummy! So, who are you going to tell?"* I turned in their direction and continued to yell obscenities, as I waited four houses down. *"DAMN! Why in the hell do we always have to get up so early, yet we're always late? Come on! Make me sick, just because of you, I'm always late for school. I should leave the both of you slow ass kids!"* I shouted, rushing my little sisters along. I grabbed both of their hands, yanking them, all while being scared of what could possibly happen to the three of us for being the only children that were walking alone to school. I urgently pulled them down the street, so that we wouldn't be late for the first bell. *"My mama always said that there was safety in numbers but for some reason, my number always consisted of me and y'all two and I'm tired of that shit!"* I continued on with my rant, *"... and yet, here we are again the only ones walking to school alone on this dark, cold and grey October day. What if someone tries to kidnap us and kill all three of us? Well, not me but the both of you! Cause' I'm going to run"* I continued. *"She knows she could have taken us to school, then we wouldn't be late!"* I was furious that my mom didn't take us to school, I definitely took it out on my little sisters. *"We telling on you, cause' you keep cussin' and you said you was going to let a man get us and kill us!"* My sister's screamed but I continued to ignore them and continued with my rant. *"...but of course, she had to stay home to take care of her baby. She needs to stop having all of those damn kids!"* I shouted. *"Yuck, that stinks!"* Said Catrice. *"...and If you try to leave us, I'm going to tell my mama on you and you make us sick too! Don't she Alisha?"* Yelled Catrice with both hands on her hips, while she rolled her neck and popped her lips at me. I yanked her hand even harder and pulled her down the street. It took everything in my power not to leave them, especially Catrice. As we were walking, I stopped to look up to the heavens with my hands together and prayed as loud as I possibly could. *"Lord if you can hear me, please make my mama stop having all of these kids. I should have been the last one, I don't even like them that much! For real and I'm sick and tired of walking them to school! I have a life too you know, Amen!... I said Amen! ...[looks down at sisters]... Can I get an Amen? (little girls voice saying amen)The smart talking one said, 'Amen!"* I exclaimed. *"Boy are you stupid!"* I laughed. I always had to walk my younger sisters to school and it was beginning to get the best of me. Although, we were not that far apart in age, our personalities differed and it was very noticeable. The youngest of the two was rather quiet but that *damn* Catrice, the eldest of the two, talked entirely too much. I didn't care about what she said, plus she was always talking too much and meant what she said, that she'd tell on me. I

didn't care though, my only concern was to not get chased by

any of the many animals that frequented the neighborhood, *you*

know the lions, tigers and bears of the Westside. Most

importantly, I needed to get to school and that wasn't because I

liked school or anything like that. I had something in my

backpack, that I'd felt would grab the attention of the kids who

never talked to me. Something I could be respected for and not

teased or taunted, like they'd normally done to me. I had my

sister's Shay's most prized possession and I just knew it would

give me the social boost I'd needed. *"Chief Indian Summer,*

where did all that warmth go?" I thought to myself as I placed

my hands in my pockets to keep my fingers warm, the weather

was shifting. We continued to walk carefully pass the homes

that had cats or dogs, I was terrified of anything that had a tail

and four legs. *"Come on... now!"* I'd sternly whispered to my

little sisters. I could sense that things were about to shift, I

knew those dog owners always let their animals do whatever

they wanted to and I wasn't trying to get ate. I tried sneaking us

passed those houses without being spotted but it was a little too late. *"Oh my God!... RUN!"* I screamed, alerting both of my little sisters. There was a giant German Shepherd quickly running towards us as if he was in a dog race. I then pointed to a car in the distance and we quickly ran towards it. As we got close to the car, I picked both of my sisters up one at a time and swiftly threw them onto the hood. *"CLIMB UP TO THE TOP, SO HE WON'T GET YOU!"* I screamed as they continued to cry out for help. This instantly made me flash back to the time I'd sacrificed Michael to Mrs. LeShea's German Shepherd, many years ago. *These damn Nazi dogs had it out for me!* When I jumped onto the car in an attempt to get away from that vicious animal as he tried to consume us, I couldn't quite grasp or find my grip on to the hood. I just kept sliding off. This had to be due to the type of material of my clothing and me moving around so fast but I didn't give up. Once I was finally able to stop sliding from the vehicle, I positioned myself on the roof. The German Shepherd continued to run around the car barking and trying to jump on it to eat us. In a panic, I threw my book bag as hard as I could at the German Shepherd, to scare him off and it worked. My book bag hit him straight in his face. It must've hurt him because he ran off and not only did he leave, he also stole the very backpack that just struck his face. My sister Shay's most prized possession was in that book bag and if that wasn't an omen of what was to come, I don't know what was. I continued to try and calm my little sisters down but they were really shaken up but suddenly, I heard an old faint voice in the distance. *"Get the hell off of my car!"* There was an elderly woman looking out of her front door faintly screaming, *"Romo, Romo... Get in here right now!"* She yelled for her dog continuously. That German Shepherd stared at me, as he held onto my backpack with his jaws locked and ran back to the elderly woman, wagging his tail while she held her front door open. This dog, which had tried to eat us and who had stolen from me, was well received by his elderly owner without any disciplinary actions. As she anticipated him running back into the house, when he got to the door she grabbed my book bag from his mouth and held it up in the air . *"Come and get this bag!"* She yelled, *"... And get off of my damn car, NOW!"* The Elderly Woman maliciously commanded us to get off of her car. *"Is that your dog ma'am?"* I asked, *"You do realize that*

241

you shouldn't let him out because he might bite somebody!" I screamed but that didn't phase the Elderly Woman. *"I said come and get your bag or are you hard of hearing? Bad ass kids, come and get it right now!"* She yelled back at me but I didn't appreciate the way she was acting towards the whole matter. *"Then keep your damn dog in the house! He could have killed us and I'll come and get it, only if your dog is locked up."* I frighteningly replied. *"Then come and get it or else I'm going to keep it."* Stated the Elderly Woman. *"Can I please have my book bag your dog stole from me?"* I screamed as I attempted to help my little sisters off of the car, but they were still too frightened and they wouldn't budge. The Elderly Woman continued to defend her vicious dog, as if he was some type of puppy or something. *"... But my dog didn't steal anything from you and I shouldn't give your little fast ass shit! You could have damaged my car and you better shut that big mouth of yours before I let him back out!"* She yelled before throwing my book bag out onto her front lawn and slamming her door shut. My heart was beating so fast, I thought that it would explode right through my chest. *"You freaking witch!"* I

242

yelled, while looking behind me to make sure she didn't release her dog again. *"Come on! Stand right there, I'm going to go and get my bag!"* I walked carefully over to the yard to retrieve my belongings and more importantly, my sister Shay's most prized possession that I had borrowed. I turned to look for my little sisters and seen that they had crawled back onto the car, too afraid of the possibility of that stupid dog coming back. I tiptoed back over to the vehicle and helped them off of the car once again. *"Are y'all ok?"* I asked with concern, because they were crying and scared to death. I know right before all of this happened, I had a small rant about my little sisters, *hell*, I'd even prayed for them to go away but the truth was, I did care about their safety. They were in my custody and were my responsibility, so I couldn't and wouldn't let anything happen to them. *"I want to go back home! Is she gonna let her dog back out to bite us if we get down? She said she was, I want my mama!"* Cried Alisha. *"Don't be scared I'll protect you. I didn't let that mean old lady's dog bite you, did I? No, I didn't! So, don't ever be scared! I won't ever let anything hurt you, I'll die first!"* I passionately stated while still being a little nervous from what happened. I had to be strong for them, I was the big sister now. After I got them down, I grabbed hold of both of my little sister's hands and placed them in my pockets, so none of us would be cold. I briefly looked over my shoulder to make sure no harm was secretly approaching us from behind, as we continued our journey to school. Despite the way I'd hollered at the both of them, I loved them and I'll be dammed if I let something or anyone harm them. *"DAMN!"* I screamed out loud, the cold made me forget about us almost been mauled to death by a ferocious animal. *"If you keep on cussing like that, I'm going to tell my mama on you! Plus, you told God you wished you didn't have no little sisters, so I am telling my mama on you!"* Said Catrice. I couldn't believe after all of that, she still was going to tell. *"... And after I saved your life? Man, you've got some nerve! Whatever, I don't care what you say or who you tell, it's still cold and I will cuss all I want. SHIT, GODDAMN! Now go and tell that!"* I shouted as we continued walking to school. *"The warmth was just here last week and now it has departed like a thief in the night. I should have let your fingers freeze and fall off with your smart ass mouth!*

That's why my mama doesn't like you and she is going to give

you away to the gypsies!" I teased, as I pushed Catrice through

the door of the school. We made it right before the tardy bell

rang. At this point, I had forgotten all about the dog, the cold

and that damn tardy bell. None of those things bothered me

anymore, because it was the perfect weather for what I had

worn.

The hours seemed to pass me bye, as I sat at my desk with the

palms of my hands touching my face and my fingers tapping

the sides of my temples. Despite being almost mauled on the

way to school, this day had been amazing. It was even better

than when I wore my cousins high heel shoes to school and she

never found that out. I began to brush the bangs out of my face,

huffing and puffing as I continued to daydream about every

single moment of this very day, and whatever was to come of

it. I continued basking over the events of the day and nothing

could take that joyous feeling away. Not the stupid pop

quizzes, surprise spelling test or anything could take the place

of how I was treated for having my sister Shay's most valued possession... her jacket. *"I hate school!"* I mumbled to myself as the other kids played and ran around the class. School was almost over for the day but it seemed as if it were taking the bell a little longer than usual to ring and I knew that I needed to haul ass when it did. I was anxiously awaiting the perfect time to leave, I knew I was going to face some consequences for what I had done that cold and faithful morning. I had created the perfect storm for myself, all for recognition and to be acknowledged. *Now don't get me wrong*, I love the beginning of what I had done, *in fact*, I basked in the pleasures of it all day long. The weather surely cooperated with me but now, the countdown was on. I was free and clear to leave without those little pesky sisters of mine, because my mom had picked them up as usual. I continued to think to myself that I should have never done what I done. *"Oh, how I wish that I could go back and change the hands of time but I can't."* I stood next to my desk. My hands were sticky with dirt and sand from being outside, they were also covered with strands of hair that hugged the lent from my pockets and from me trying to fix the wildness of my hair, all of the candy that I placed in my mouth

246

and ate, while licking my fingers clean on the playground. I looked down and my legs were even ashy from the boys chasing me and my new found friends. *That's right, I finally had new friends because of this magical jacket.* All the horse play that I'd participated in during recess had me looking a bit wild and a hot mess. There was sticky bugs on the side of my sweater, my shirt hanging out of my skirt, my bangs flapping down over my eyes with my two wild pony tails trying to break free from the rubber-bands that held the hairs on my head hostage. My socks rolled down, unable to stay up because they were full of candy and *Now & Laters*. I even spit in my hands to wipe the ash away from my knees. This was a great day but I had to beat my sister Shay home, before she knew I'd taken her magical and mystical jacket. My feet began to move without my brain telling them to, you would have thought that I was about to run the 50-yard dash in the Olympics or dance and throw the scarf in the air and *jit*. I'd grown beyond impatient, I could feel my heart beating out of my chest and resonating like African drums within my ears. I stood up and began to pace back and forth next to my seat. My teacher, Mrs. Smith began to speak as I continued to fidget. *"Now quiet down class otherwise you will be here until 3:30 and you miss Kimberly must take your seat! Did you hear me Kimberly? Take your seat!"* She yelled. *"Oh, hell no I won't!"* I mumbled to myself. *"What did you say Kimberly?"* Mrs. Smith asked as she walked in my direction. *"If you thought you were having problems quieting the class down now, wait until they gather around me when I start to shake and convulse on the floor."* I mumbled. *"Keep playing with me Mrs. Smith if you want to! This shit ain't no joke, this is real life! A matter of life or death... my death."* I thought. I could feel a scream building up on my insides, ready to pry open my lips and sing the *Help Me Hallelujah Jesus* song. I could feel my spirit about to go into the holy ghost in the very next moment, if I weren't able to get out of there. The students in the class continued to make noise and get out of their seats, including me. However, I had a very good reason for doing so. *"I said, remain seated!"* Mrs. Smith exclaimed, as she banged on her desk with a ruler to gain control over the students and obtain order in her classroom. I looked around in anger at the kids in the class. *"I know one thing they better sit there asses down and now!"* I screamed inside my head. See, the kids in my class had no idea that I wronged my sister by taking one of her prized possessions, that magical *yet* all powerful jacket of hers and that she got out of school at 2:15. If I didn't get home before my sister Shay, there would be hell to pay and... I was just not prepared for it. I knew that if the teacher released us right at the sound of the bell I could make it home in time to place all of her things back, because my older sister school was a couple of miles away and she walked home with her friends. She usually wouldn't get home until about 3:30 but something seemed a little off today, so I knew that I needed to get out of this damn school immediately. I sensed this was an omen with that *damn* German Shepherd trying to eat me, *I should've payed attention to the signs.* Finally, the first bell rang and Mrs. Smith called us by rows to go to our lockers to retrieve our belongings.

"Damn!" I exclaimed. *"I hate school, she ain't gone never call our row! Would y'all please shut up, dang!"* I shouted. After seeming like a million years, Mrs. Smith finally called the third row, my row. The killer part about everything was, Mrs. Smith

decided she was going to try something different on this day. Instead of calling our row only, she decided to call us by name. *"Marcus, James, and Kimberly go to your lockers grab your belongings and absolutely no talking!"* Mrs. Smith stated. I jumped up out of my seat nearly pushing Marcus and James out of the way, hurrying to my locker to retrieve my wraps and the very article of clothing that did not belong to me... but for today, this very day, it was mines! I grabbed my wraps, returned back to the classroom and was the first to stand in line and wait for the teacher to dismiss the class. I looked out the window and could not believe my eyes. The omen of that old elderly witch and her devil dog, was revealing itself. *"NO! No ... no, it just can't be?"* I shook my head vigorously from side to side. *"Is everything all right?"* Asked the teacher. I quickly nodded *"Yes!" yet* still in disbelief of what I was seeing. *"Well then take your seat or you will be here after school!"* Stated Mrs. Smith. I continued to ignore her, *first of all she wasn't making me stay anywhere and I had to go!* I turned and looked out the window, I couldn't believe my eyes. It was snowing and I knew good and damn well that the weather guy said clear skies, otherwise I would have never...

[*school bell rings*] *"Ring... then twice... ring, ring ...then*

thrice ...ring, ring, ring." Mrs. Smith held her finger to her lips

as if to quiet us all and said slowly, *"Class... dismissed!"* I

quickly grabbed my books and ran towards the door. I pushed

that door so hard, that it slammed up against the bricks outside

of the school. I immediately ran as fast as I could until I made

it to the first corner. I was making great strides, when all of a

sudden, the safety patrol boys put their hands out and said.

"STOP!... WE SAID STOP!" I couldn't believe this madness.

First of all, I was in the fifth grade now and secondly, I didn't

need anyone helping me to cross the street. That was for the

kindergartners and the first or second graders. I pushed passed

those two safety guards as they tried to grab me and started

running again. They both hollered in unison, *"YOU'RE*

GOING TO BE IN TROUBLE, CAUSE' WE KNOW YOUR

NAME, KIMBERLY WADE! JUST WATCH WE'RE GOING TO

REPORT YOU, WITH YOUR UGLY BUTT!" I wasn't thinking

about them or their threats. That was just something I couldn't

worry about, I had to get home. It was imperative that I made it home before Shay, so let the cards fall where they may and I will deal with it tomorrow. *"Unless, there is no tomorrow."* I thought to myself, as tears began to stream and blur the vision of my eyes. I lived approximately 6 ½ blocks away from the school, if you counted the side street that the school sat on. I just had to beat her home, her middle school was further down but who knows if she got out earlier. It was snowing and to top it all off, her magical and all powerful jacket, her most prized possession was becoming all messed up! *"This is some straight up bullshit!"* I continued to run until I reached the second block from my street. I bent down with my hands on my knees and my hair all over the place, hoping to catch my breath. After taking two quick breathers, I began to walk briskly. I was walking so fast that I couldn't retain the air that I tried reserving, I needed to rest again. *"Maybe I can get home in time enough to throw it in the dryer."* I thought to myself. I began to walk faster with urgency, almost in a run with my breathing still labored [*stares into the distance*]. *"NO! That couldn't be."* I shouted, I thought I'd seen my sister Shay in the distance. You would've thought I'd seen the ghost of Christmas future, coming to take me away. *"Could this day get any worse?"* I instantly ran down the street as fast as I could, soaking wet from the snow that had turned to rain. I turned and looked back over my shoulder, that ghost was becoming more visible. *Was it that damn ghost of Christmas future?* Nope, it was her... my sister Shay in the flesh. She along with one of her friends, spotted me and started pointing in my direction. *"Hey, Shay... isn't that your sister? Nice jacket she's wearing."* Her friend solemnly stated. *"WHERE? CAUSE' I KNOW GOOD AND DAMN WELL SHE AIN'T GOT MY JACKET ON!"* I was caught, I didn't know how to get out of this one. *"KIM! YOU GOT ON MY JACKET? I'M GOING TO KILL YOU WHEN I CATCH YOU! YOU'RE DEAD KIM! DO YOU HEAR ME? YOUR ASS IS DEAD!"* Shouted Shay. At that very moment, I knew that If she were to catch me, I would be a goner. I thought that I could make it home, break back into her bleak yellow suitcase and place the jacket back. Then when she took it out to wear it, I could deny that I had ever touched it, because that stupid suitcase was kept locked anyway. *How could she prove it?* Especially, if she locked all of her stuff up but no!

Her stupid friend just had to open her big ass mouth. *"I SEE YOU AND I KNOW GOOD AND DAMN WELL, YOU'RE NOT WEARING MY JACKET!"* Shouted Shay from down the street. *"I'M GOING TO KILL YOUR ASS, JUST WAIT UNTIL I CATCH YOU!"* She continuously yelled. I was completely out of breath but I continued to run as fast as I could, passing the very street that I lived on and almost falling flat on my face. *"Oh, my God! She's really going to kill me!"* I cried. In fear of being caught, I turned once more and looked over my shoulder to make sure she wasn't behind me. That didn't work to my advantage, I could hear her off in the distance *yet* that distance was getting shorter. I could hear her thunderous voice getting louder and louder, she was gaining momentum and began to catch up to me. I ran even faster, one would've assumed I was being chased by a pack of wolves. That German Shepherd's omen was revealed and I was racing for my life but that would mean nothing to my sister, I had made an unforgivable mistake. Shay had managed to turn into something I couldn't recognize, some sort of monster out to devour me. The faster I ran, the faster she ran in an effort to catch me. I ran even faster in my

254

quest to get away from the wrath that she would bestow upon my weak and frail body and all of this because I borrowed her new magical and all powerful white jacket from her locked suitcase, that she kept her most precious and valuable items. I had to borrow it against her will and against my better judgement, because had I asked her nicely, *"Please can I wear your jacket... pretty please with sugar on top?"* Shay would have looked at me with her hands on her hips, while rolling her neck and eyes and in a loud thunderous voice say, *"HELL NAW! You must be crazy if you would ever think in a million years that I would ever let you wear anything of mines! I can't stand you, so why would I let you wear my stuff? I don't even like you!"* So, asking her was just out of the question, at this point it wasn't even an option all of that was out the window. This jacket was beautiful, magical and mystical, so white, so pristine, locked away in that dingy yellow dungeon of a suitcase. I'd freed it from that daunted abode and was able to allow it to grant me my wishes of friendship. *I failed to mention to you all, how I was able to do this.* When I released that beautiful jacket from the wrath of the other items that were being held prisoner, I took a safety pin and began to pry open the prison that held her captive, I would release this beautiful princess from the dungeon if it were the last thing that I would do, not realizing the trouble that I was getting myself involved in. I had to do this and it worked! I jiggled that safety pin around a couple of times as my fingers began to hurt and boom, she was finally free from the clutter of all the other things that Shay had locked away in that dungeon suitcase. *"I think I will call her Marilyn!"* I stated as I twirled around with the jacket swinging freely from the breeze of my spins. I waited in the closet for my sister to leave. I peeked around and called out her name softly then abruptly, just to make sure she was gone. *"Why are you calling your sisters name and that loud, you're going to wake the baby, plus she's already left for school. Where you need to be going right now!"* Stated my mom, as I secretly placed the jacket in my book bag. Fast forwarded when I was able to get away. *"Ma, I'm about to go."* I told my mother, as I began to walk out the door. *"No, you're not! not without these two and where is your coat?"* My mom asked. *"Dang! Why do I always have to take them to school? They walk to slow, that's why I'm always late and my coat is in my bag, I'm hot!"* I said as I walked out of the house. *"Come on, cause' I'm not going to wait!"* I said as I pushed them both out of the door, and down the street. *"That's why I'm telling, you stole her jacket when we get home!"* My little sister Catrice stated smartly. *"That's why I should leave your ass right here where your standing, I can't stand you anyway!"* When we'd arrived at school, I dropped the both of them off to their perspective classes and I was afraid that someone would pick on me, push me or something. They were always picking on me but to my surprise, all of the girls who had never spoken to me before came up to me and talked to me and they wanted me to sit with them at lunch. They all liked the jacket, one of the girls even invited me to her party over at her house, it was a last minute decision on her part but I didn't care because I wanted friends and plus, she said Michael Jackson was going to be their because he happens to be her cousin, *so we must've been cousins too!* I wanted friends so bad, but just didn't know how to make them. I received rave reviews by wearing that magical white jacket. This was a game changer for me, I was shy and I felt like if I'd dressed the part, everyone would like me. So, I had to do it! It's deep, really deep and the reasoning behind me breaking into my sisters belongings and stealing, *I mean borrowing the jacket.* I have now reached the point of no return, and I must be about to die because they say when you're about to die your entire life as you knew it flashes in front of your face and I'm remembering too much about this morning, plus I can't even breathe and well, my sister continued to chase me down the street. Not knowing where to run, I turned and ran as fast as I could down the first alley I came to. Tears streaming down my cold, rain and sleet-soaked face. I had no idea that it would rain like this or mix with the snow and turn that beautiful white jacket into a flat cloud of grey. I'd ruined it, just so people would be my friends. I continued to run as fast and as far as I could get, I needed to get away from her and I couldn't stop. *"I SEE YOU AND I AM GOING TO TELL MY MAMA ON YOU... BUT NOT AFTER I BEAT YOUR ASS FOR WEARING AND MESSING UP MY NEW JACKET! JUST WAIT UNTIL I CATCH YOU!"* Shay shouted as she continued gaining on me but of course, she would kill me and I knew that it was going to be painful. I had

to share a bed with her and she wouldn't even let me move

without punching me as hard or as many times as she could.

"Oh, No!" I cried out loud, I could feel her cold harsh breath

on my neck. Shay caught me by the arm of the jacket and

swung me around, then let go. I slid across the grass on my

stomach and all of her friends began to laugh. They watched as

Shay mercilessly continued to beat me up. *"TAKE MY*

JACKET OFF NOW!" She yelled as she pulled my arms out of

the jacket and pulled the jacket over my head so I couldn't see.

"What am I going to do, SOMEBODY HELP ME?" I

screamed, trying my best to get away from the brutality that my

sister placed upon my body. *How will I explain this misdeed to*

my mother, after she believed that I was just too warm to where

a coat. I hated lying and disappointing her. *How could I have*

done such a thing? Just to see the disappointed look on her face

would torture the very air that I breathed for my entire life.

This was not a joke but I couldn't go back there, I just couldn't.

I could never, ever go home because she was going to tell and

when she does, I'm going to get a whooping and I don't want

that. *"I'm going to tell my mama on you!"* I cried as I tried to snatch away from my sister but she continued to swing me around. *"Lord, please help me get out of this situation, if you could find it in your heavenly heart!"* As I continued fighting my sister off and trying my damnedest to get away, I continued praying. *"I will go to church each and every Sunday and some days out of the week, without my Grandma or anybody else telling me to be quite and whooping me to make me go... and oh yeah, I'll be good in Church and my Grandma won't have to pinch my arms or threaten me after giving me peppermints or chewing gum to be quiet. Oh yeah and God, that is if you are listening to me, I won't take the money I get from my Grandma to put in that bowl, that those people with the white gloves on and the one hand tied behind their backs while taking everybody's money have, who by the way tried to take my money. You know God, they actually take too much in my opinion but I will never forget to put the money in the bowl anymore. I promise I will not keep it for candy, Amen!"* My body had gone limp and began to fall but my sister wasn't having any of that and she began to punch me repeatedly on my legs and arms really hard. *"THIS IS FOR TAKING MY JACKET!"* Screamed Shay, as her friends continued laughing. I tried to get away but couldn't, so she grabbed me up by the jacket and held on tight *"OH YEAH, YOU'RE GOING TO GET IN TROUBLE FOR MESSING UP MY JACKET!"* She shouted, continuing to drag me home. I was kicking and screaming, dreading getting the whooping of my life, by whomever was there to do the deed. I continued hollering and biting and fighting. *"LET ME GO! I SAID LET ME GO! YOU GETTIN' ON MY GODDAMN NERVES! YOU PEANUT BUTTER MUTHA FU... {LOUD PUNCH} ...!"* That's as far as I got, my words had been abruptly cut short. Shay punched me in my leg so hard, that I was silenced and couldn't walk. Shay then dragged me the rest of the way home.

When we got home, we both ran in the house talking at the same time. *"I didn't do nothing and Shay beat me up in front of her friends!"* I cried *"... And Kim, stupid butt wore my new coat and messed it up. I never wore it!"* Shouted Shay. *"I DIDN'T WEAR HER JACKET"* I cried loudly. *"Then explain*

261

why you have it on Kim? Make me sick!" Shouted Shay. *"I*

DON'T CARE BECAUSE I'M LEAVING ANYWAY! CAUSE'

NOBODY DON'T WANT ME HERE ANYWAY!" I cried.

Needless to say, this went on for the duration of the night into

the next morning.

The next day came and I was on my way out the door for

school. My sister Shay stopped me and said, *"You might as*

well have that jacket, cause I'm never wearing it again! I don't

want it because you funked it up, your dirty butt!" I looked at

her and said. *"Well, give it to me then!"* Shay threw the jacket

and it hit me in the face before hitting the ground. I bent over

picked the jacket up, took my coat off and put that magical

jacket back on and continued to walk to school. So now you

know, just why I was running for my dear life in the beginning

of this book. It was all for that magical white jacket and even

though I took a beating from my sister, it was well worth the

rewards. *SQUARE BIZ!*

GRADUATION

The day had finally come for my days in elementary school to finally be over. I'd completed the sixth grade, was about to graduate and *you know what?* A couple of people like me and want to be friends. It took years for me to have friends in school but it had finally happened. That magical jacket really helped me a lot. I hadn't been bullied in a while and that felt great. I remember my mom buying me a dress, some sandals and a memory book for my graduation. I remember when the Principal called my name, I was filled with joy and so elated . *"Kimberly Wade!"*... *{auditorium erupts in cheers}* ... I walked across the stage with my hair flowing down my back, my yellow and white striped dress and my white wedges. The Principal shook my hand, gave me my diploma and a dictionary! *That's right, a dictionary.* I stopped an accepted that dictionary with pride and said, *"Thank you!"* and proceeded to walk across the stage.

Can you believe it? Me, the person who was bullied, then bullied others, who skipped school, who was held back and who passionately hated school because of racial prejudice and discrimination, was able to accomplish the goal of graduating. How happy was I, to have cake, ice cream and hotdogs with the very people who I'd once called my enemies. *My, how the tables have turned! I guess it was just another day in my life of ...Elementary, My Dear!*

Now middle school, *what can I say?* It was the best time in my life! Unlike elementary school, I never wanted to miss a single day. *So much for me hating school, right?* Middle school was the time that I'd actually came into my own. I loved school, I had no worries about any bullies. I even remember my first day (*McFadden & Whitehead's "Ain't No Stoppin' Us Now" was even playing on the radio*), I had on some corduroy pants with the slits on the side and some glass heal shoes. *Oh yeah, I thought I was the shit!... {laughter}... but that's another story.*

To be continued...

ABOUT THE AUTHOR

Author K. Bethany is a Foundational Black American novelist/playwright who honed her passion for writing in Detroit, Michigan. At a very young age, K. Bethany started to develop a niche for great story telling. From the many writing contests she entered as a child, to some of her great essays written while studying law at Wayne State University. K. Bethany has written several books across various genres of literature including, romance, crime, drama, suspense, horror and even comedy. K. Bethany looks to turn all of her literary works into theatrical adaptations as well as tv sitcoms on various streaming platforms. With continuous drive and creativity, K. Bethany looks to bring to life her many stories of triumph, love and excellence to inspire many generations to come.